AND THE MONEY

WENT OVER

THE RAILING

How a Dutch Survivor from

WW II Found a Future in the U.S.

James Vanderpol

Order this book online at www.trafford.com
or email orders@trafford.com

Most Trafford titles are also available at major online book retailers.

Printed in Victoria, BC, Canada.

ISBN: 978-1-4269-2340-1 (sc)

Library of Congress Control Number: 2009913765

*Our mission is to efficiently provide the world's finest, most comprehensive book publishing
service, enabling every author to experience success. To find out how to publish your book, your
way, and have it available worldwide, visit us online at www.trafford.com*

Trafford rev. 12/29/2009

Trafford
PUBLISHING® www.trafford.com

North America & international
toll-free: 1 888 232 4444 (USA & Canada)
phone: 250 383 6864 ♦ fax: 812 355 4082

PREFACE

Life takes interesting and unexpected turns. Many years ago, my brother bought an Apple Computer and gave me his old Microsoft machine. I had no knowledge of how to use a computer and decided to use it as a typewriter and write my autobiography. I showed my 250 pages to various literate friends and all insisted that I polish the text and have it published. I somehow delayed my decision to act upon the advice until age 85.

The main reason for writing an autobiography is based on the many speeches I gave primarily to students, but also to adults. My talks were about my life's experiences including growing up in the Netherlands where I lived in a positive and loving environment until the age of 15 when I was thrown into an extremely brutal and cruel environment—the Nazi occupation which lasted for 5 years. I did survive and came to the United States in 1946.

The purpose of my speeches was to stimulate thought about "what makes us a truly responsible person", including facing the responsibilities of each citizen to make a democracy work. I asked each listener to send me a letter responding to my speech and, although there was always a remarkable interest in what I had to say, the subject, for most of my audiences, had never been really considered. I would like to pass on my legacy to anyone interested in the hope that it may be of some benefit.

ACKNOWLEDGEMENTS

Over 18 years ago, my brother gave me his old computer. Faced with a useful purpose for his gift, I decided to write my life story. Folders of pages emerged, but in spite of encouragement from family and friends, the transformation of raw material to a living book languished.

Last year, Kathy Levine marched up to me during church coffee hour and said "When are you going to publish your autobiography?" Standing close by, Ann Clough added, "I will retype, edit and polish it for you, and I found to my utter amazement a project was born.

After all this effort, I needed help to format the typed pages for publication. I asked my former very able assistant at the United Way, Gail Evans, and she was most willing. Last, but not least, my wife Carol and our daughter Anne brought their literary skills to the effort. Many thanks to all of you.

CONTENTS

Preface   v

Acknowledgements   vii

My Life in the Netherlands   1

World War II   14

My New Life In The United States   43

College Years   52

Touring our New Country   59

Starting Work at Hart, Inc.–Boston   65

Coopers and Lybrand–Boston   75

Coopers and Lybrand–Pittsburgh   80

Coopers and Lybrand–New York   91

Family and Community Life–New York   95

Huntington Hartford   105

Becton Dickinson   128

Bennington College   147

Bradford College   174

Emerson College   182

Retirement   206

My Life in the Netherlands

I was born in July, 1924, in Amsterdam, the Netherlands. My father, Joshua, informally called Joe, was a wholesale diamond merchant and had a business in Amsterdam and in Antwerp. He was well respected in the industry and had built up his business from scratch. He spent part of the week in Antwerp and part in Amsterdam. Sunday was spent with the family. My father came from a lower middle class family and had educated himself after finishing grade school. He originally wanted to become an actor as he was blessed with a beautiful voice, a knack for storytelling and good looks and charm. He was a stern man, but a good entertainer both at parties and at home. Certain stories of his from his time as an amateur actor became classics in our family. His role as a father took on aspects of a Supreme Court justice. Because he spent little time at home, my mother used the approach of "Wait till I tell your father!" which usually did the trick. We had great respect for him. He never spanked us, but one reprimand from him and we froze.

My mother, Rachel, most often called Rae, also came from a middle class family. Her father, Simon, was a rather simple man who had narrow views of the world and made a marginal living as a diamond cutter. To supplement this income, my grandmother, Griet, started a millinery shop and worked long and hard. My mother in her youth helped my grandmother and, because of this, became rather knowledgeable about hats. Many years later, when she was married, she bought a hat and showed it to my father. He didn't like it. So my mother took a pair of scissors and narrowed the brim. My father still didn't like it. In desperation, she went back to the store and persuaded them to take it back and exchanged it for a new hat. Her powers of persuasion allowed her to do some wondrous things in the war and later on when she lived in Flushing, NY.

My mother was very close to her mother and revered and respected her. She was always quoting her. I was impressed with my grandmother's deep understanding of life and human behavior. My mother inherited some of that and was always helping family members who were in some kind of trouble. She told us many stories about her youth, some of which were very funny. She had two brothers, one of whom was a practical joker. When they were young, they had a live-in maid who had been with them for many years. On Friday, her fiancé would come, and she would become anxious long before he arrived. My uncle Raph connected a wire from the toilet to the front door bell. He would sit on the toilet and ring the bell and the poor maid would run to the front door to find there was nobody there. I don't know whether she ever figured out my uncle's trick.

Every year, my great grandmother would knit for the grandchildren. My uncle had heard that, one particular year, she was knitting underwear for his birthday. He told his mother that he would not wear it as it was too itchy. She told him that, out of respect for his grandmother, he had to wear it. He refused. When he actually received it on his birthday, he refused again. He was told that he would not get dinner. A week went by without dinner and he did not complain. The following week my grandmother received a note from his teacher to ask her to come to the school. The teacher told her that her son was a wonderful boy. He had admitted that his father was an alcoholic and had spent all the money so that there was not enough food at home. In response, the teacher had taken a collection and wanted to give the money to my grandmother. Needless to say, my uncle was grounded for a considerable amount of time.

Some stories about my family are included here to provide a fleeting look at some of the people who influenced my life and to show the love and closeness in my family. This brought a sense of security and comfort to me. This does not mean that there were not the usual family squabbles. One of the more amusing ongoing tensions existed between my two grandfathers. Each Sunday evening, my grandfathers and my mother and father would get together to play bridge. My father had a natural talent for the game, and my mother worked hard at it, but my grandfathers told each other every Sunday night what the other did wrong. Many times they left angry at each other, but they were always back together the next Sunday.

My father was an impressive man. He was good looking, a sophisticated dresser, and a good story teller with a beautiful voice of operatic quality. On Sunday morning, he would spend hours in the bathroom and sing excerpts of opera. Some Friday nights, we would have a musical evening with my grandmother playing the piano and my father singing the latest songs from Paris. He could be a stern man, but had a good sense of humor. He told us many stories about his experience as an amateur actor. He once played the romantic hero in a love scene in the living room with a beautiful chandelier. The next scene took place in the middle of a wild ocean. My father was rowing and trying to save the heroine. Unfortunately, in the fast change of scenery, the stagehands had forgotten to remove the chandelier. However, the story that I liked the most was when his fellow actors played a joke on him. In the play, my father was to stand over a wishing well and recite a long, romantic poem. Only then did he discover that his colleague had put some cow droppings in the wishing well. My grandfather was a very strong man and, if any play went beyond 11 p.m., he would climb onto the stage and carry my father off the stage so that he could get home and be in bed on time. In the end, my father decided not to pursue an acting career, partly because the family considered acting to be an unacceptable career.

When my father was engaged to my mother, she complained that he had forgotten her birthday. The next year, he hired a band and, at six o'clock in the morning, the band played happy birthday for her and, at the same time, to my mother's embarrassment, awakened the whole neighborhood. She did not complain again. They were married on a boat decorated with red roses, floating down the Amstel River.

Since my father was only home on weekends, much of the discipline was left to my mother. She was rather free in slapping us when necessary. My father never did use physical discipline, but one look at him would keep us in line. I remember my mother as a warm and generous person full of life and very people oriented. She helped a lot of people over some rough times. She was also usually the life of the party. One time, as a young girl, she was in a private school and apparently did not like the woman who was the principal. One day when the principal was away, there was a ladder in the school courtyard and, during recess, my mother climbed the ladder and mimicked the principal. She didn't realize that the principal had returned and was seeing the whole show. My mother never told us what her punishment was!

On Sunday, we usually took a long walk with my mother. My mother believed that walking was good for us. So, on many Sundays, we walked all over Amsterdam. She knew a lot about the city and pointed many things out to us and that made our walks very interesting. However, what was more interesting to us was that we usually ended up at one of my mother's favored aunts, Tante Leentje, who always had something good for us to eat. Once, the three of us were on a streetcar in Amsterdam, and my brother Ries and I did not behave. My mother was angry and slapped us. We cried. A lady on the streetcar commented that my mother should not be so severe with us. My mother made no comment until we got home and then she gave us a double dose, this time on our rear ends.

One concern of both of our parents was that they wanted to make sure that we accepted a strict work ethic. In addition, we were to be strong and independent. When I was in my teens, my mother and I were going by train from Amsterdam to Rotterdam. The train was always very crowded. This time my mother told me that, as the man, I should be more aggressive and make sure that we both got a seat. When we got on the train, my mother forgot her instructions and took me by the hand and pulled me through two cars before she found two seats. What she had not realized was that, in the melee, she had taken the hand of a stranger, while I walked quietly behind the man through the two cars.

My father considered religion a crutch for the weak. He was humanistic in philosophy, but strongly believed in the idea that a person should stand on his own feet and work and fight hard to be a success. My mother was totally influenced by her mother who came from a Jewish family and, although she didn't go to temple, was deeply religious. My mother respected her faith, but she never went to temple or instilled a strong sense of religion in my brother and me. I did feel the need of a church affiliation as I experienced the tragedies of World War II and will talk about that later.

We were not affected by the depression of the thirties as my father was a prudent business man, and we lived a financially stable but modest life. I went to Montessori kindergarten. The only thing that I remember from this experience was that I watered the plants in the classroom because I was a good boy. This behavior changed in later years. When I started elementary school, my mother was called by my teacher. She was very concerned about me because, in the twenty years of her teaching experience, she never had a student who insisted on starting his notebook in the middle rather than on the first page or the last page. My mother had more faith in me and was not concerned. I don't remember much of what I learned in school except that people considered me a brain since I could add, multiply, divide and subtract in my head. There was no secret to this as the teachers drilled you endlessly in the fundamentals of mathematics.

One of my formative experiences centered on music. My mother had taken piano lessons due to great pressure from her mother. My mother put up a sustained resistance and finally my grandmother surrendered. Later on, my mother regretted that she had not continued her studies as she loved music. She decided that, if she had children, she would insist that they would learn to play the piano. So, my brother and I were put to the task. My mother's position was further fortified by the fact that our aunt, Tante Jo, was a piano teacher and needed the money to support her family. I started when I was about 7 years old. I fought the idea until was about 13. I developed several techniques to convince my mother that it was not for me. My mother would sit every day with me at the piano to make sure that I practiced from 4:00 to 4:30 pm. I tried to move the clock 15 minutes forward to reduce the practice time. She got wise to that. My most creative resistance was that I found a dog that did not like certain tones and would go into a high pitch whining. That didn't last too long either. I had a lesson each week, and I would cry after my aunt laid a guilt trip on me because I had not studied according to her instructions. However, suddenly I discovered that I enjoyed it! Since then, I have continued my studies and appreciate my mother's willingness to put up with me during the six years of grief.

I had an inquiring mind which led to some complications. In those days, the milkman delivered milk from house to house. The milk was not in bottles but in a tank, and the milkman would take your pan and fill it. I was honored to become the assistant to the milkman, but was under strict orders not to fill the pans on my own because the faucet on the tank was not like an ordinary faucet. With my inherent urge to learn about the unknown, I tried once to do it myself. The milkman was busy talking to my mother as they both liked to talk. However, I quickly realized that I did not have the talent to close the faucet. The milk started to pour into the street while they were so busy talking that they still did not notice. In my dismay, I did not take remedial action and watched the street become a beautiful white milk stream. Needless to say, when it was discovered, I got appropriate punishment that I do not want to detail!

Another learning experience happened one day when my brother and I went on our bicycles to a nearby canal. Amsterdam has more canals and bridges than Venice. This particular canal often had lumber tied together for raft-like transport down the canal. Unfortunately, when I saw one of those "rafts", I jumped off my bicycle and onto the raft. I then realized that the raft was untied, and I went under. That was dangerous. I was a good swimmer, but the lumber closed over my head. Fortunately, my brother took quick action and pulled me out. We now had to devise a plan to dry my good clothes and evade my mother who might notice the dirty water on my outfit. We decided to bicycle until my clothes were dry and, when I got home, I would go straight to my room with the excuse that I had a lot of homework. This worked beautifully until, at bedtime, I made the mistake of folding my clothes. This aroused the suspicion of my mother since this was a complete change in my usual handling of my clothes. It didn't take long for her to get to the truth.

A more mischievous incident involved scaring my grandfather's girlfriend. My grandfather had been a widow for some time and invited a lady friend to our home. At that time, he was living with us. She was a loudmouth and had an unattractive appearance. She always came on Thursday afternoon as my father was not home and my mother played bridge. She had the habit of going to the downstairs bathroom at about 4:00 pm. One Thursday, I engineered a contraption in the bathroom with a string from the doorknob to the toilet cover which was in the upright position. Another string went to the faucet, another string connected to the flusher, and the last string connected above the door to a little pail which, upon opening the door, was positioned so that it would turn upside down to let the water fall on her head. This was not an easy feat. After I had rigged this together, I had to open the bathroom door to get out without disturbing the various traps inside. It was a rip-roaring success when she made her 4:00 visit. She was overwhelmed by the noise and the splashes of the water. Also, since my father disliked the woman, my grandfather could not tell him what I had done because she was not supposed to come to our house. Later on, I felt sorry for what I had done, but I think that my grandfather's romance would have died a natural death in any case.

Another stunt centered on my mother's bridge addiction which led sometimes to late or meager suppers. To remedy this, my brother and I were able to connect an upstairs speaker to the radio downstairs so that we could talk into the speaker and our voices would be broadcast downstairs. On Tuesday, the bridge club met at our house. Late afternoon, we reported that one of the ladies had a fire at her home and that somebody had called the radio station to announce it. We were hoping that she would hear the broadcast, but the ladies were so busy playing bridge and talking that we had to repeat the message three times before we heard any reaction from downstairs. In this case, my mother never found out what we had done until much later.

I actually had a wonderful childhood and a good family. There was a strong sense of roots and closeness between so many relatives. My mother had a difficult task playing the role of father and mother as my father was really not home enough to play a day to day role with us. This was in the thirties and, in general, the father was seen more as a breadwinner and not as a guiding light for his children. It was not customary for the father to do anything in the household. We had a live-in maid. One day when she had the day off, my mother asked my father to help her with washing the dishes. This was a courageous request. To her surprise, father said yes. She had used the Sunday dishes as we had had some dinner guests. When she handed the first gold plated washed dish to my father to dry, he took it and dropped it on the stone floor. He said, "Well, I thought so! I am not talented enough to do this". Then he left the kitchen. What he really wanted to do was to tell my mother that she should never ask him to help in the kitchen. Times certainly have changed!

My brother, who is a psychiatrist, helped me understand why my mother drilled into each of us her idea of how we should live. This was an unconscious effort which resulted from putting the sum total of her upbringing into the instruction of her children. She was very effective as a mother. However, it was sometimes hard for us to realize how well she had conditioned us for life. The more lasting characteristics were to be considerate and philanthropic. We must also be strong in character and have strong work habits. We were meant to succeed in anything we would undertake. "Hard work never kills anybody." A strong component of all of this was a great respect for education. If I did not do well in school or in sports, I felt very guilty to the point of being scared that the world would crash in on me.

I was a good student, but not exceptional, and this was also the case with sports. Of course soccer was the main sport, and every free moment we would gather on a field and use jackets, coats or sweaters as the field goals. Then, someone would assume the leadership and divide us into two teams. It was always interesting to me how someone would assume the leadership and how others, including me, would accept it. It didn't always work that way and, when that happened, that would lead to quarrels or fights. We still had a good time.

Another pastime was canoeing on the many canals. We had a canoe and, since I used it the most, I invented some interesting games. Once, a friend Bob and I bought water pistols and squirted each other in the canoe until the canoe was totally flooded and capsized. Whoever stayed the longest in the canoe was the winner. This went on very well until one day we saw some huge water rats staring at us and that ended our interest in canoeing.

I referred earlier to the method of learning in the earlier years which involved the endless drilling in the fundamentals of what was being learned. This also applied to the learning of Dutch, French, German and English with an elective additional language in the upper grades. The final language exam in high school required the student to be able to discuss four books in each language using the respective language, as well as passing a written examination. The one language that I didn't master very well was German. I had a high school teacher who was a highly respected German philosopher who taught German to make a living. Each year, he offered the class a choice: to learn German on the honor system by reading your assignment without him checking, while in class he would lecture on Goethe, the great German poet; or, learn the language in the traditional way. Every student chose the first option as it meant less pressure. Usually, after three weeks, he lost everybody with his deep insights about Goethe; but, since our assignments were not graded or checked, we felt that we had a good deal. It is interesting that most students prefer the easy way without realizing that they lose out in the long run by not learning anything.

One excellent teacher was our history teacher whose assignments really made us think. He would describe a certain problem in the past without giving the names of the people involved. Our assignment was to suggest how we would solve the problem. After we had done this, he would then explain how the problem had actually been handled at that particular time.

In general, however, the Dutch educational system was based on terror. There usually was no easy rapport between teacher and student and, since parents emphasized the importance of education, a student's fear of not doing well was enormous. If a student failed more than two subjects out of the fifteen or so you had to take, the student had to repeat all the subjects for that year. Students who failed again were dismissed from the high school. Education in the Netherlands was severe and, in general, parents would put a lot of pressure on their children to do well.

As you progress through the grades, the fear builds up. The reason is that, once you reached the twelfth grade, you had to make far-reaching decisions. The choice was to go to a high school that specialized in languages and commercial subjects or a high school that concentrated on the sciences. If you did not qualify for either one, you could go to a three year high school and, if that was too difficult, you might qualify for the advanced elementary school. There was also a school for the true geniuses called the Latin School. All of these schools put a stamp on you for the rest of your life. The Latin School curriculum included four languages, plus Latin and Greek, and all the sciences. Usually, not more than twenty applicants qualified; half of them would be forced to drop out during the six years at the Latin School. I attended the literary/commercial high school, which is a five year school. The problem was that, at the end of each year, you had to pass thirteen of the fifteen subjects that formed the curriculum; otherwise, you had to take all fifteen subjects again. At the end of the fifth year, you had to take a final examination in all the subjects with questions covering all five years. This exam was one week written and one week verbal. A representative from the Department of Education attends the verbal portion to make sure that the teachers ask the proper questions. Really scary!! Apparently the system has changed drastically. Another problem was that there was no easy communication between the teacher and the student. The teachers were formally dressed, and the principal walked around in a cut-away suit. On reflection, I don't know whether the amount of learning I received from this education justified the great fear of failing.

One teacher terrorized the whole school. He taught geography, a required course, and intimidated all his students. If you did not pay attention in class or if you did not do your homework, he would ask you to step in front of the class. He then would grab your ear and pinch it with his nails. However, he was an extremely knowledgeable man and, if you did your work, he would praise you. As a result, everybody tried to stay on his good side. The final challenge was his final exam. He would blindfold you and give you a letter opener. You would select one page from the four textbooks you had studied. He would then say, "You have selected page 40 from book two", and he would ask you questions about that page. Normally, you had a week before the finals to prepare. Most students spent half the time on geography and the other half on all the rest.

Another noteworthy teacher was our English teacher. He was hated by just about everybody. He had the habit of keeping you after class, and would give you a note for each deficiency he had noted. These included talking in the class, not paying attention and poor homework. You had to take his notes home and have them signed by a parent and, for each note, you had to do extra homework. I had accumulated five notes. I was the last one after class to be given the notes. When he handed them to me, I noted that he gave me four. I made a calculated decision to play it straight. I said, "Mr. Harder, I deserve five notes". He looked at me and said, "Are you pulling my leg?". I said, with a straight face, "No sir. My parents taught me to be honest". He was so impressed with my actions that he tore up all my notes. Honesty paid off, even with Mr. Harder. I still disliked him intensely and got my reward when, sometime later in the year, I waited after class until all students had left and Mr. Harder was still in his class. I had obtained a key to his room and locked his door from the outside and left the key in the lock so he could not open it from the inside. Apparently, he had to stay there a long time until somebody came to the rescue. My fellow classmates had some idea that I had done this but, with all the threats Mr. Harder made to find out who had done it, nobody ever squealed.

Some of my high school experiences were even more humorous. One required subject was drawing. We had a teacher named Mr. Maandag (which in English means Monday) who was a very nice man, but a very poor teacher. His greatest problem was that he could not control the students too well, and he was also accident prone. I had no talent in drawing pictures. My greatest achievement was to draw Snow White and the seven dwarfs with enough resemblance that people could identify them. Therefore, I sympathized with a classmate named Fritz. He was not born to sit in a classroom for any length of time and was absolutely lacking in drawing talent. Because of the lack of artistic skills, he constantly was in trouble with Mr. Monday, which meant that he had to do extra drawings as a regular punishment. In order to relieve this situation, he arranged to have fellow students make drawings for him. One week, he was out of drawings. He had to come up with at least one. He said, "Don't worry. If I have to stay up all night, I will produce a masterpiece". I knew that there would be a calamity and there was. The following day, Mr. Monday asked Fritz to present his drawing. Fritz presented him with a rolled up paper with a ribbon around it. The classroom was built like an amphitheatre so we all could watch Mr. Monday unfold the paper. He looked at it, then turned it upside down and looked again, then sideways and looked once more while his frown was getting deeper and deeper. He then turned the painting to the class and asked if anybody had any idea what it was. What we saw were big circles with ever smaller circles inside and a dot in the middle. After some guessing, Mr. Monday asked Fritz what it was. Fritz answered that he was surprised that a man of Mr. Monday's talent could not readily identify it. He said that this was a picture of somebody looking out of an airplane at thirty thousand feet over a stadium. The dot was the field and the circles were the seats.

Mr. Monday told him to stand in the front right corner of the room for the duration of the period. Unfortunately, that corner contained a little basin and a water faucet and, behind Fritz, was a big detached closet. After a few minutes, Fritz got restless and opened the faucet. When it overflowed the basin, it formed a stream of water which was heading straight toward Mr. Monday's shoes. He was concentrating so intently on giving his lecture that he didn't notice that we all were staring at what was happening on the floor. Suddenly, he looked down and noticed that his feet were wet. He turned and walked upstream to get Fritz. Unfortunately, Fritz had fled around the corner of the closet, and now the steeplechase started around the closet. The class made noises like an audience at a horse race. Some were even shooting spitballs at the ceiling. Then the door opened, and the principal stood in the doorway. He was, as usual, dressed in a dark suit and held a bowler hat in his hands behind his back. He stepped forward. In the sudden silence, one could hear a pin drop. However, just when he was about to say something, a spitball crashed into his bowler. Because of the complete silence, the sound of the spitball sounded very loud and made us all laugh. However, the principal did not. He left the classroom and, later on, we were told that Fritz was dropped from the school and that the class was suspended for one day with serious extra homework and a note to the parents. I think that it is universal that students can be very cruel to a teacher who really is not equipped to handle a particular age group. This was really sad because Mr. Monday went out of his way to help if asked.

On balance, I got a very good education. When I went to college in the United States, I could coast for the first two years and still make the dean's list consistently. The last year of high school, I was segregated into a separate school because the Nazis had taken over and, since I didn't qualify as an Aryan under Hitler's rules because I had Jewish blood, I was considered unclean. It did not make much difference because, by that time, the whole educational system was falling apart, one of the reasons being that all textbooks were censored. In particular, history books had been reduced to a few pages as the rest was considered not in line with Hitler's philosophy of fascism. The school system was also affected by actions of the Nazis to "purify" the language and eliminate any Anglicism. One example of this was that any use of the word "stop" must be changed to "halt", not only in our textbooks, but also on all street signs.

WORLD WAR II

My experiences during World War II, which for me fell between ages 15 and 20 (May 1940 to June 1945), are a sharp contrast to my life before that time. My youth was a happy one. I had friends from various religious persuasions. My best friend Jan, a Catholic, had a mother who was Catholic and a father who was Dutch Reformed. Religion in our friendship never played an important role. It is interesting to note that in a book I recently read, written by an Englishman about the history of Amsterdam, he repeatedly brought out two main characteristics of the Dutch: tolerance and the desire to make a profit. I think that my parents gave me a good foundation with a strong sense of family and caring for your neighbor. This certainly helped me to face the unbelievable hardships my friends and I had to endure. It saved me from insanity and total despair. I never lost faith and had a strong feeling that right would prevail. These are some of the experiences I would like to share.

Shortly before the Nazis invaded the Netherlands, Hitler had called our Queen Wilhelmina to say that, no matter what happened, he would not invade Holland. Not long afterwards, his troops marched in. On Wednesday, I had read in the paper that the Dutch army was going to have some massive war exercises and that the population should not be alarmed. My father was, as usual, out of the country. On Thursday, planes were flying all over Amsterdam, and we heard the noise of cannon fire. We looked out the window and saw pandemonium with people in nightgowns screaming that the Germans had invaded. I reminded my mother and brother of the newspaper article about the Dutch army war practice, and we went back to bed. Very soon thereafter we found out that the Nazis had started invading our country, Belgium and France. We had a formidable army, we thought, of about a million men. The country had a food reserve for four years, and it also had a system of flooding specific sections of land to drown an enemy. As is now well known, all the allied countries had completely underestimated Hitler in his preparation to conquer the world. It was done with typical German thoroughness and, of course, the Nazis justified their consistent lying and other amoral behavior as actions done for the good of the fatherland. History teaches us a lot. However, we do not necessarily apply the lessons learned. Hitler and Nazism were made possible through the impossible harsh conditions the Allies set up for Germany after World War One. These conditions created such post war misery that Hitler, with his promises and his emphasis that Germans really were superhuman beings, could succeed in leading his countrymen to war.

One example of the German thoroughness was the use of cleaning maids as spies. It was customary in Holland for middle income families to have a maid. Each year, the cost went up and the pool of Dutch maids got smaller. Some years before the war, many German girls came to Holland and offered their services as maids at a much lower wage. Many people took advantage of this new source of domestic help. What we didn't know was that many of these girls were organized by the Nazis to spy on us. It was done in a very clever way. They told the girls that, on a regular basis, they had to send a letter to a post office box in Germany. They should write about anything they heard. They didn't have to screen the information. It was more like writing to your family about recent events. The Nazis would take all this information and sort it out. In return, the maids received an allowance in Germany for their services. This is one of the reasons that it took the Germans only five days to conquer the Netherlands. They were so well informed that they knew the whole system of flooding the various areas and, in many cases, the Nazis were able to get to the controls first and drowned Dutch troops. As another example of their preparations, early during the five day war they flew in a horse and carriage, accompanied by a detachment of paratroopers who were to take over the palace of the Queen. They would force her to ride in the carriage through the streets to show that the Germans had taken over and won. However, the son-in-law of the Queen, Prince Bernhard von Lippe-Biesterfeld, who was of German origin, defended the Queen and the family with the palace guard and was able to help the whole family escape to England. To do this, he had to fight his own brothers who were part of the German army.

After my family and I realized that the war had started for sure, we went into something like shock, outwardly cool, but inwardly totally overwhelmed by the circumstances. We concentrated on trying to get through to a resort hotel where we had made reservations for a long weekend. We didn't consider that, because of the war, all reservations were obviously not going to be honored. We then concentrated on our basement to make that a safe shelter. We had no idea where my father was. Later we found out that he had tried to return to Amsterdam, but could not make it because of the German's rapid advance and because all roads were totally clogged. My father, like most people, thought that, with the help of the French and the English, the Germans would soon be defeated. How wrong he was! He stayed in the south of France and eventually moved to the United States and lived there until the war was over.

We talked to family and friends and were hindered by a lot of wild rumors, making it difficult to make useful decisions. The main concern was whether we should try to flee and, if so, where. Our best friends decided to go to Zandvoort, which was not far and was a beach resort. Supposedly, there were fishermen who would take you in their boat and bring you to England. That actually happened, and many fishermen did help people – primarily Jews who didn't have faith that the Allies Would come to their rescue in the near future. Unfortunately, there were also some stories of boat owners who would acquire passengers for an outrageous price, take them halfway across the channel to England, and then throw them overboard and go back for a new load. War sometimes makes bad people worse and good people better. I saw this over and over again. As war creates extreme conditions, people tend to react more in the extreme.

We decided that we would stay in Holland and hoped that our father would come to the rescue. We had been Dutch citizens for generations, and the Nazi propaganda machine was already broadcasting that they would not interfere in our country and that the Dutch were really kinsmen and brothers of the Germans. Little did we know what the future would hold? At the age of fifteen, I thought it quite exciting. First of all, I didn't have to go to school as it was closed for a while. Secondly, I ignored the advice to stay in a shelter as I was busy watching the dogfights in the air. They were so spectacular that you almost forgot that there were people in those airplanes. My curiosity almost cost me my life as a part of a plane landed very close to me. I didn't see it coming or hear it. One unexpected learning experience was thrust upon me when I was called, as a Boy Scout, to duty as an auxiliary to the National Guard. I had to visit families and inform them that a husband, brother or son had been wounded or killed. At fifteen, I grew up in a hurry! When I delivered the verbal message, some started screaming at me. Some did not say anything as if they could not really grasp the message. And, some realized that I was a young boy and treated me accordingly. I don't remember too much about that period. I know that money was an issue as that was usually handled by my father. We were able to open the safe deposit box and found a number of Dutch gold pieces. In normal times, they were worth approximately ten dollars. Within a short time, their value went up to ten times as much as nobody accepted Dutch money because of the war. The gold coins actually helped us to get through the war financially.

The Nazi occupation tried to convince us that they would not interfere with our daily life. Of course, the uncertainty about what lay ahead for us was like an albatross around our necks. The war news was awful. It became very clear that the allies were so poorly prepared that it was very clear that Hitler had won the first round. I was blessed throughout the war with an undying faith that good would prevail and that I would survive. Meanwhile, the schools had reopened and slowly we saw the impact of the Nazi propaganda. We didn't know who to trust and; therefore, became a little more careful in what we said. The teachers at the high school tried very hard to act as if nothing had changed in order to reduce our feelings of anxiety. Ironically, the only known Nazi sympathizer was our English teacher. He was a Dutchman who had lived in England and didn't like the English. This was not surprising as he was a strange man who was uncomfortable with people. It is interesting to note that, in general, in Holland, people who became active Nazis were the kind of people who had so far failed in life or had suffered a terrible youth, which left them with pent up hate. It also became clear to me that people, who on the outside were constantly advertising that they were successful and staunch churchgoers, many times had no courage, drifted with the wind and certainly did not fight the Nazis. In the beginning, there were many people who wanted to fight the Nazis, but wanted to have a certain amount of recognition for that among their friends and acquaintances. These were not the people who really were the mainstay of the underground movement as the one most important rule was to keep all your actions as quiet as possible as the Nazis were extremely well-trained in spying on everybody.

The nature of the different cultures was revealed clearly in the way the news was broadcast on the radio. The Nazis would have five minutes of drumbeats and then they would announce the latest victories. The English, through the BBC, would report the news as dry and sober as if it was a stock report. Later on, the Americans would broadcast, and the reports always bordered on sensationalism with some secret weapon that would shortly be used and would end the war. Our choice was to listen to the BBC as they proved to be the most factual. Their broadcasts gave me a sense of hope as they created a sense that they knew what they were doing and that they had the strength of character to face the tremendous difficulties ahead.

I should mention that it did not take long for the Nazis to declare that listening to any allied radio station was to be punishable by death. We had to be ingenious to develop ways to be able to listen to a foreign radio station. We bought a little crystal radio and used the transformer on our bicycle to create enough electricity to power the crystal. One would sit on the bicycle and peddle and listen secretly to the radio. We would hear the German propaganda minister, Goebbels. The man was a genius for lying, bending the truth, and couching his pronouncements in such a form that you had to think twice to figure out what the lies were all about. Even children's books were rewritten substituting Hitler for the book's hero. In addition, the Nazis consistently exaggerated their successes in military battles. The tonnage of ships that they claimed to have destroyed during the war bordered on the ridiculous. We divided the tonnage by a factor of five to ten and figured that to be more accurate.

Since my family members were considered undesirable Jews, we slowly came to anticipate the upcoming restrictions and eventually recognized the threat of death. The Nazis had very detailed rules as to who qualified as an Aryan. In order to qualify, a person had to have three parts out of four non-Jewish heritages. It seemed that the Nazis had a million rules for all the variations. A milestone occurred when they announced in February, 1941, that all Jews had to wear the Star of David on all their outerwear. Dockworkers, streetcar conductors, and utility workers went on strike in sympathy with the Jewish citizens. This was the first overwhelming public expression that the Dutch had no use for the Fascist ideology. From then on, the Nazis showed their true colors more and more and implemented one of the cruelest governments imaginable. Its cruelty really exceeds comprehension.

Star Of David

The Dutch had a four year food supply. This was taken by train to Germany. At the border, they would put signs on the railroad cars explaining that this was a gift from the Dutch to the German Reich.

Food rationing started. In the beginning, this rationing was not too onerous, but eventually became harsher until, in the final year of occupation, we had one rotten Polish potato as a total week's ration. At that point, everything was obtained through the black market or through barter or through our underground forces stealing special rationing cards from the Nazis. Of course, the Germans had enough food for themselves and the Dutch Nazi sympathizers. When the war was over, we found substantial quantities of food in the places where they had lived.

Some ingenuity also helped to relieve the situation. I had heard from a friend that, if you had ulcers, you could obtain special rations. A doctor friend explained that, if you drank a lot of coffee and stayed up all night before you went to the German Health Board, you could stick a needle in your finger and suck the blood so it would eventually show up in your stomach. If you did that, you would create enough symptoms that the doctor would conclude that you had an ulcer. I went through this exercise and did it so well that the doctor could not understand that I was still alive. I did get the extra rations, but I did not do it again!

In war conditions, a whole society changes dramatically in its habits and in relationships between human beings. Because of the ever-increasing, deteriorating conditions, one can see much clearer how people deal with adversity. In extreme conditions, there is not much room for a happy middle ground. You either cope well and honorably or you do not. That is why it has been said that war brings out the best and the worst in people. As I write about my experiences, I will relate some stories about other people that illustrate these points.

As the Nazis, through their new occupation government, started to interfere with our lives, a new experience of fear entered our lives. For Jews and other enemies of the Reich, restrictions started to add up. Schools became separated; all public buildings and parks were off limits to us. We were not allowed to use any public means of transportation. Fortunately, the common way for the Dutch to get around was the bicycle. This became an even more precious commodity. To guard against stealing, people would take the bicycle inside the house and even chain it to their bed at night as thieves became more audacious in their stealing. The undesirables also had to surrender all radios to the

Nazis, and jobs were not available to us. The Nazis continued to try to convince the Dutch that their idea of a society was superior to ours and that it was an honor to be considered part of the superman society. The Dutch, as a whole, did not buy it and consistently resisted every move the Germans made. Nevertheless, a sizable group went along with the Nazis. There were many reasons for this such as fear, power, and the effective way that German propaganda used the most primitive instincts of men to hate, to lust, and to succumb to the herd instinct.

We used whatever means were available to cope with the situation. We found that, for unknown reasons, the profession of house cleaning exempted you from being transported. I don't remember how long I was a house cleaner, but I do remember that I had to get up at an ungodly hour and then bicycle to the other side of Amsterdam to the office that would give out the daily assignments. I would then bike all over Amsterdam to do the different jobs that I had been assigned. Since I was totally inexperienced at this kind of work, I dreaded the various housewives who gave me instructions and then inspected my work.

Later, opportunities for work were tightened by the Nazis, and the cleaning job was no longer exempt. It also became more and more unsafe to be out on the streets as the Gestapo started to become more and more visible in taking Jews and other undesirables away. My first attempt at going "underground" in 1942 was at the apartment of two elderly spinsters who were family friends. My brother and I stayed there for awhile and had no particular problem coping with this new situation. We still had enough food and heat and light to live comfortably. We also spent some time with a favored cousin in a country house. I almost got killed there, not because of the Nazis, but because a bolt of lightning hit the house and then cut an old tree in half as I was standing outside watching the beautiful lights in the sky. I had a kitchen knife in my hands, and next thing I knew, I had a severe shock as the lightning went through my body and then sparked through the knife which flew out of my hands. I then felt that God was watching over me and that my time had not yet come to die. After staying there for awhile, my brother and I moved to Wassenaer, near The Hague. A prominent socialite bachelor was living in an imposing house. He was very friendly—too friendly as it turned out. One night when I had gone to bed, he sneaked into my room and started to touch me. I just pushed his hands away and, fortunately, he got the message. However, we left shortly thereafter.

Things deteriorated rapidly for everybody but, for us, it was really serious as the German and Dutch Gestapo started to raid homes and pick up Jews and other enemies of the state. I was now in serious hiding at various places. My family had a group of close friends who were of the Christian faith and, unsolicited by us, showed their friendship by risking their own lives to help us. Most of the deeds done to help us were punishable by the death penalty. There were so many Dutch enemies of the Reich that the joke went around that 50% of the Dutch were hiding with the other 50%. Through our friends, I found new hiding places and food and received communication from friends and family. I stayed with one family where the father had been jailed and sent to a camp in Germany. He had been fighting in the Dutch underground and was caught. Each Christmas, the commandant of the German camp sent one of his fingers to his wife. She never wavered in her faith and said that she would continue what her husband had started in the underground and she did. Once, when I stayed at her house, she had a visit from her minister. He asked her for advice as he had been called upon to join the German army. Germans used most of these recruits as front line fodder in order to save the German men. The minister asked her if he should go and spread the gospel as best he could among the Nazis or go in hiding. The lady looked at him and said, "I am disappointed that you even ask that question. If you think that I will give you comfort by helping you to rationalize your decision to join German troops by saying that you are going to spread the gospel, the answer is no! You are really afraid of the Germans and want an excuse!" He did follow her advice and went into hiding. She survived the war, and her husband did return, but had lost most of his fingers due to the barbaric treatment by the camp leader.

Deportation Center

Transport Line Of Deportees

Meanwhile, around 1943, conditions deteriorated rapidly for me as the Nazis started to concentrate on what they called the ultimate solution which was to eliminate all Jews and other undesirables. I moved to Scheveningen, a beach resort between The Hague and the North Sea. A couple in their late fifties, who lived in an apartment, took me in. This was a very brave act on their part because, if the Nazis found me, they would be shot as well. The landlady lived in the upstairs apartment. She was an old spinster who apparently lived like a recluse. In those days, you could not take any chances because she might be a Nazi sympathizer. My staying with the family downstairs created a problem as the landlady visited the first of every month to collect the rent and to inspect the whole apartment to see if it was in good condition. For the approximately two and a half years that I lived there, each time she visited, I would stay one room ahead of her when she made her inspection. She always moved through the rooms in the same sequence. Shortly after the war, she came for her usual visit, and I introduced myself and told her that I had been there all that time. I will never forget her face. She was not a Nazi sympathizer but, as I said, you really could not take a chance and trust your neighbor. The family I stayed with had two grown children. One was a delightful daughter who helped us in many ways; the other was a son who was not very sure that his parents should take that risk for me. I will not use their real names, although they are no longer alive. I will call the parents Mr. Peter Holland and Mrs. Lena Holland. Mr. Holland had a senior position with the Dutch government. She had enough backbone for two and any doubts that he would raise during the years that I was there were quickly erased by Mrs. Holland. I observed all throughout the war that women, once they made up their minds, seemed to have more tenacity and endurance than men. Mrs. Holland was a good example of that, and my mother was also. Later on, I will relate some of the many heroic things they did.

After I settled in at my new hiding place, we made various preparations for our safety. Through the underground, I got new identification papers. Since my appearance was pure Germanic as some of my forebears were non-Jewish, I did have some general advantage of not being recognized as a Jew. The next thing was to build a hiding place within the apartment in case the Gestapo raided the house. These raids increased in frequency and intensity as the war went on. In the guestroom where I slept, there was a chimney. About twelve feet up, we carved a space of sufficient depth and height so that I could stand in it. We had a ladder in the chimney so that I could climb the ladder to the space and then pull up the ladder and hide it also inside that space. This way, when the Gestapo used a flashlight to look up the chimney to see if anybody was in there, they could not see me and, with no ladder in sight, they had no clue that I was there. As the Gestapo got more sophisticated in their searches, they would enter the house usually by kicking in the front door at night and then run to the beds and feel if the sheets were warm. If they were and nobody was in the bed, they knew that somebody was hiding. I had organized my bed with two top sheets so that I could pull the bottom sheets out and leave the cool top sheet undisturbed. This took a considerable amount of practice, but I had the whole exercise down so that I could fix my bed and get in my chimney in less than a minute and that actually saved my life. Even so, it would have been too much time if they had easily forced the front door open. However, Dutch houses are well built and it didn't work like a Hollywood movie where you open the front door with your shoulder.

People were creative in designing indoor hiding places. One place where I stayed had an attic. In the attic were two bins with a movable partition in the middle. One bin was filled with potatoes and the other was empty. In the empty bin, there was a loose panel in the floor that led to a hiding place between the floor below and the attic. If a raid took place, we would slide through the entrance in the floor, the landlady would close it and then lift the movable partition so that the potatoes would roll into the second bin and hide the entrance. This was especially important as the Gestapo would look for unusual seams in the floor to discover hiding places. The other problem was the use of bayonets. The Gestapo would cut through the furniture or floors with their bayonets to see if there was anybody hiding inside. I didn't have that experience, but I know of a case where four people were hiding between the floors and a bayonet hit one of the people. The others quickly put their hand on the victim's mouth so he could not scream. However, they had to wait too long for the Gestapo to leave, and they had to watch the man bleed to death.

I was saved once because of Mrs. Holland's determination and courage. One evening the SS knocked on our door. They didn't knock it down. Mrs. Holland opened the door. There was no time to warn me as I had already gone to bed and didn't hear the knock right away. When Mrs. Holland opened the door, she asked what they wanted, and they said that they wanted to search the house. Mrs. Holland stood in the middle of the doorway and said that she would not let them in as they had no right to do this. They could not believe what they had heard and started to scream that she had to step aside. She held them up for a few more precious moments. Because the German language is quite loud normally and because of the screaming, I was able to get out of the back door since there was not enough time to get into my hiding place. I started to climb over the fence but, when I got onto the top of the fence, I noted that on the other side was a glass greenhouse. I had no choice but to climb over the roof of the green house. I promptly crashed through the glass, but I just had a few scrapes. I knocked on a neighbor's door, and they let me go through the house without asking questions. I was then able to run through the dark streets to an emergency hideout at another location. What saved me was that Mrs. Holland, with her remarks to the SS, got them so angry that they were screaming at her and apparently didn't hear me crash through the greenhouse on the other side of the fence. Many times the SS or Gestapo treated women with some restraint. If it had been Mr. Holland at the door, they would have shot him right on the spot. This might have just been my experience and not a general behavior pattern. If you were known to be anti-Nazi, then shooting someone down, whether male or female, was a normal occurrence.

One sad, but sort of humorous, story went around about a man hiding from the Nazis. I can't vouch for its authenticity, but it told the story of a man who had a hiding place in a house under the floor in the bedroom. A year went by and nobody had searched the house. Then, one day the Gestapo came. The man went head first through a hole in the floor, but got stuck half-way because he had gained too much weight during his stay. The lady of the house told him not to move and put a sheet over his rear end which was sticking out. On top of the sheet, she put a plant and made the whole thing look like a little table with a plant. The Gestapo didn't notice the peculiar table as she kept talking to them the entire time that they were in the house. Thereby, she managed to save his life.

During this time of hiding, I was basically confined to staying in the apartment. I had good identification papers which were produced by the underground, and it was hard to distinguish them from the ones issued by the Nazis. Since I looked like a German, I would have a better chance to be unquestioned by the many patrols that would stop people on the streets. The trouble was that people my age were subject to the draft as noted previously. You had to have an exempt job, which I didn't have, to avoid the draft. Later on, the underground got so efficient that they actually stole original blank identification papers and rationing books from the government. At one point, they had a bigger supply of these than the officials.

In the beginning of my confinement, I tried to read books each day in three different languages–Dutch, English and French. This was possible as the family had an extensive library. I helped with the cleaning and other household jobs. At night, I would play a card game called KunKan, which was a form of gin rummy. This was Mrs. Holland's favored game. It became fairly monotonous after playing it so regularly. To spice it up a little, I started to cheat with the cards and tested how much I could get away with. I learned to take three cards from the deck instead of one. I also talked to her to distract her, and soon, I could almost control who would win.

As conditions deteriorated, my life became more difficult. Food became more and more of a problem. In the last year of the war, the official rationing was one rotten potato for the week and that was all. We had to rely on the black market and on barter to get some food. Meanwhile, back in Amsterdam, my mother was also forced to barter for food. This meant hours of walking in the snow, rain and cold with an empty stomach. We were all totally undernourished. She was at risk of being robbed by others who might take her food. In addition, since my mother was an attractive blonde, she was also at risk of being stopped by the Gestapo. However, she was brave and successful and helped many people to stay alive. One day, my mother and a lady friend went with a pushcart to a church where they distributed potatoes. On returning, a wheel got stuck in the streetcar track in front of the SS building. The SS guard saw them struggle, and he came to the rescue. After he got the wheel unstuck, my mother said to him, "You are crazy to stand around in the cold while Hitler is drinking Champaign". He laughed sheepishly and went back to his post. I was able to receive some of the food that she had collected, delivered by friends who were in the underground. Recently, I read in a book, which dealt with the suffering of the Dutch people, that never in the history of the western European countries had there ever been such a methodical starvation process as the Nazis instituted to punish the Dutch for their ideology and for resisting the war effort. In the last year of the war, we were forced to eat almost anything that had some nutritional value. This included horse and dog meat and meat from other animals, but the most common food was tulip bulbs. They tasted like French fries, but were hard to digest. You could almost feel them travel through your digestive track. Many people could not digest the bulbs at all.

In the last year of the war, everything became scarce. We had no electricity and only a few candles. Matches were hard to come by as they were not made in Holland. We had no warm water or soap. During that year, the Nazis built a V2 missile station nearby. They shot a missile toward England every twenty minutes. The trouble with this process was that the missiles were launched from ground level like a bullet from cannon. When the missile reached a certain height, it would level off and an internal engine would take over to guide it to its destination in England. Parts of the engine were made by slave labor, and every slave worker tried to sabotage them. The result was that we had to listen to see whether the engine would start when it was well into the air. If it did not, it would come straight down to earth. Fortunately, the explosives were controlled by a timing device and would not explode on impact. However, the danger came from the sheer weight of the missile and its contents which were quite substantial. On New Year's Eve of 1945, a missile fell in our block. The air pressure broke some of the windows in our house. We couldn't get any window glass, so we used boards to cover the window.

In addition, we had no heat for the house or fuel for cooking. We just had to do without heat. However, somebody invented what was called the miracle stove. This was a metal can with holes pierced in it for air intake. It required very small pieces of dry wood, which we obtained by using chairs, other furniture or anything made of wood. Some houses ended up having no staircases left or other basic things. The next problem was getting the fire started. Paper was scarce, and matches were even scarcer. If you couldn't get a fire started, you couldn't eat that day since there was very little food that one could eat raw. My life was now totally dictated by such circumstances. Since we had no artificial light, we lived by the daylight hours except for when there was a full moon, which often didn't help as the Dutch climate is mostly clouds and rain. At night, I would sneak out to find some wood. In the morning, we would try to start the miracle stove and use it to cook whatever we had. This could take as long as four hours as the wood often was not very dry and the fire was very small. After that, we would read if there was enough light or talk or play cards.

My real entertainment was to sit behind the curtains and look out onto the street and see what the neighbors were doing. It's amazing what one can find out that way. I had to be careful that people could not see me as I was not supposed to be there. I especially watched for our landlord because I could only play the piano when she was out of the house. The Hollands didn't have any piano music. This forced me to learn by ear. On the clandestine radio, I heard English and American jazz, and so I started to try to play what I heard. I will never forget my first try. It was an American song called Hold Tight (Want Some

Seafood Mama). They sang it so fast that I never could understand what the real words were! I had a good time at the piano, but had to be on watch for the landlady's return. After the war, she confirmed that she had never heard me.

The lack of food and other basic necessities, the fear day and night of being caught, and the realization that people where I stayed risked their life for me added up to stress that was difficult to deal with. All this happened to me between the ages of 15 and 20. Going out or having a date was out of the question. However, once a year I would go for a week to another hiding place where there were other people of my age. The last stay there almost cost me my life. It was in the summer. A mother and daughter lived in a nice apartment on the top floor of a building. Both were very active in helping people hide from the Gestapo. They also stored a lot of underground literature. When I came that summer for a week, I warned them that they really should be more careful.

There were three other young men my age that had a variety of reasons to stay away from the Germans. There was also a nurse who was Jewish, but had excellent false identification papers which would make it hard for the Gestapo to find out who she really was. We spent the day bantering and talking and, one night, we decided to have a party. We had found some alcohol, and I had bragged that I knew how to concoct a good drink. I really had no idea. I took the bottle of alcohol to the bathroom along with some spices from the kitchen. I then proceeded to mix the alcohol with water and the spices and tested the concoction. It didn't taste very good so I added a little more alcohol to the drink. What I didn't realize was that, with the constant hunger I had to live with, my resistance to alcohol was low. As I continued to experiment, I didn't realize that I was getting drunk and that was why the mix tasted better and better. When the others finally checked up on me, I was as sick as a dog and ready to throw up. They dragged me to a bedroom window and kept my head outside so that I wouldn't make a mess in the house. When I threw up, it landed on the window sill below us. What we didn't know was that the man living in the apartment below worked for the Gestapo. When we found out, we thought that he deserved this deposit. However, our landlady was more worried about him coming upstairs to yell and, in the process, finding us. She was an amazing woman, and somehow convinced him that the mess was a pure accident of her daughter getting sick. We did have a good time that night. I had a major hangover the next day. When you are constantly under such an emotional stress, it is almost a necessity to have some excessive relief.

A few days later, I had an experience that, even on reflection, is hard to believe and which had such an impact on me that I became a firm believer in a God who watched over me. We were sitting on the roof of the building one morning to get some sunshine, which we didn't get to enjoy very often since. All of a sudden, the door from the apartment to the roof opened. There were two German Gestapo officers and one Dutch Gestapo. They had used a common trick of waiting until somebody rings the front door and then, when the door was opened, they would run in, thereby not alarming the occupants.

They told us to come inside. Our group included the daughter, the nurse, and three men, including me. The mother was downstairs as she had opened the front door and was told by the raiders to wait in the living room. The others went in, but I decided to wait it out in the hope that they might forget me. I had a large sum of money in my pocket, which I was able to throw over the railing. I didn't even consider trying to get to the next roof because, if they caught me, then I had a chance of being shot on the spot. After some time, which seemed forever, the door opened again and one of the Gestapo screamed at me that they had not forgotten me and that I had better come in right away. When they interrogated me, they cut it short and told me that they knew who I was–namely, a local leader in the underground who had helped Jews go into hiding. I had no idea where they got that information, but it didn't make any difference. They informed me that my crimes against the Third Reich were punishable by death and that, at headquarters, they would question me further. I knew that meant torture and death.

I then had to wait on the sofa in the living room while they were interviewing the others. They had already finished with the nurse who, in spite of her excellent falsified identification papers and her attractive appearance, had not been spared, but had succumbed to their terrifying intimidation and had confessed that she was Jewish. The Gestapo told us that their assignment and specialty was to find Jews. The nurse and

I were sitting on the couch for hours with the Dutch Gestapo sitting watch. He didn't say much other than that he really didn't like people and only loved his dog. In a rather morbid gesture, he offered us a loaf of bread as he said that this would probably be our last meal, and he didn't want us to die hungry. The nurse had reached a mental stage where she was totally out of control and, in no time, ate the whole loaf of bread, without knowing it I am sure. I vaguely remember that I was overwhelmed too, but outwardly controlled myself. I also had not reached a real awareness that, in minutes or hours, I might be dead.

Much later, they assembled all of us and told us that we all were going to headquarters. We were not allowed to bring any belongings. Usually they would ransack the places they visited and steal any valuables and keep them for themselves. However, just before we were ready to descend the stairs, the two German Gestapo officers whispered to each other. The next thing I knew, they told another fellow and me to go back with them into another room. The Gestapo sat down behind a small desk while my friend and I found chairs. We were not sitting next to each other, but rather my chair was diagonally behind his. The Gestapo then told us that they were only interested in eliminating Jews and, since we were underground leaders, they asked us to give five addresses of places where Jews were hiding and then they would let us go free. They even promised to give us some money. They then told us, and here comes miracle number one, that they wanted us to sign a paper that promised that we would give them the necessary information in three days. Of course, they also made it very clear that they would watch us very closely and, if we didn't deliver, we would be shot. My friend jumped up and, in a rage, started to scream, "Who the hell do you think I am? Just because you fellows want to kill everybody, you will not get me to betray my fellowmen!" His rage went on and on and, obviously, the Gestapo was ready to cut us short.

Then an amazing thing happened. I had not stood up or said anything. However, I felt like some spirit was going through my body and raised my arm for me and put it on the back of my friend. He then performed an about turn in a very convincing way, pleading that he was too young to die. He did such a masterful job that they accepted his statements. We signed some papers. They took the rest of the group in their paddy wagon while we watched them through the window. We didn't see any sign that they had posted one of the Gestapo to watch us. It truly was a miracle and almost impossible to explain or to believe. After they had gone, I rang the doorbell of the people in the downstairs apartment in whose backyard the money that I had thrown over the railing had fallen. The woman who answered the door said that she had found the envelope with the money, but she wanted proof that I was the owner. I said that finding money in a backyard is unusual and only the person who had put it there would know about it. She was honest enough to accept my explanation and returned the money. My friend and I then went back up the stairs and, to be on the safe side, climbed from roof to roof as we couldn't be sure that the Gestapo was not following us. We both escaped and went back to our respective hiding places.

I was not the only one who was saved under the most unusual circumstances. We had in our family a nephew who was considered a black sheep as he wanted to become an actor and that was not considered an honorable profession in our family. During the war, he had a plan to rescue prisoners from a concentration camp called Westerborg. He learned how to run a steam locomotive and somehow got rid of the actual machinist and drove the train to the camp. This was already risky because of control points that he had to pass through. Upon arrival at the camp, he was successful in smuggling people back to the train and into the box cars and managed to get them safely back to a place where they could go into hiding. After having done this daring rescue mission a number of times, he was finally apprehended. In such a case, the Nazis would usually hold a kangaroo court and then send the offender to the firing squad. However, as my cousin was driven from the prison to the court, he was sitting next to the driver. He noticed a briefcase between him and the driver and quickly managed to make the briefcase disappear through the window. The driver upon arrival had forgotten about the briefcase and escorted my nephew to the court. It quickly became clear that the briefcase had contained the paperwork on my nephew's case. The judge didn't even have his name and therefore, in typical German fashion, released him as there were no official papers. After the war, he was honored as one of the outstanding underground war heroes and later became one of the leading actors in the Netherlands.

During the last year and a half, when hunger, fear and the relentless Nazi terror showed no sign of abatement, I had to fight hard to deal with it all. The fact of being confined without support from my family and living without most of the material goods to which we were accustomed made life more than miserable. I never gave up hope that the Allies would eventually win. The question was when and whether I and so many others could last that long. When you live with hunger, you can easily give in to your animal instincts and become totally self-centered because of the very strong inbred wish to survive. I will spare you many of the details. However, one example of what such hunger can do to those who are starving was the one and only time that bread was given out by the Swedish Red Cross. Mr. & Mrs. Holland each received one loaf. We watched her slice the bread to see if the slices were even in size. We all suffered from lack of food; and, therefore we had to exercise maximum self control if it looked like one slice might be a trifle larger than the others and try not to grab it.

A constant worry of those in hiding was the fear of getting sick. In fact, because of the starvation and lack of heat and hygiene products, the chances of many epidemics should have been high. However, this didn't happen perhaps because we were not allowed to congregate. That might explain why the span of the war years was the only time in my life that I had no colds or flu.

At my young age, my fear of getting sick was minimal. However, one day I woke up with a toothache that was so terrible that I was willing to risk my life to go to a dentist. Since I hadn't gone to a dentist during the last two years, I had to rely on my guardian parents to find a dentist. They did have a family dentist, but didn't know whether he could be trusted. However, I had no choice. I took a different set of identification papers from the papers that I normally used. The dentist didn't ask any questions and pulled out the tooth. He had no anesthetic or electricity to power the drill so he used his feet to move the drill. It was not a pleasant experience! He asked me where he could send the bill and I almost, in my anxiety, gave him the name of the people where I was hiding as well as the name that I was currently using. I was fortunately able to lie my way out of the situation and gave another address where he could safely send the bill without compromising me or my benefactors. On reflection, I think the dentist must have been trustworthy as he must have noticed the confused statements that I was making.

The Nazis relentlessly pursued their terror as it became more and more clear to them that, even with all their propaganda, the great majority of the Dutch people had absolutely no use for their super race theories or fascist philosophies. One major demonstration took place in September 1944. It was called "Dolle Dinsday" (Crazy Tuesday) and, on that Tuesday, the Dutch railroad workers went on strike. This took place as the Allies started their attack on Arnheim in order to cross the Rhine. The workers went on strike to help the Allies, and they stayed on strike until the end of the war. This was yet another reason that the Nazis tried to starve us–in order to break the strike. According to the statistics, there were approximately 140,000 Jews in Holland, of which about 20,000 survived. Other segments of the population fought back effectively, particularly the Catholics who were well organized to fight the Nazis and also the Protestants, especially in the Northern provinces. Many people gave their lives as members of the underground. These were mostly people who quietly supported the underground out of a deep conviction of the rightness of their cause. They didn't need praise or recognition. One of the main requirements in the underground was to keep your mouth shut. My theory was that, since they didn't do it for the glory, they didn't have the need to impress anyone. Therefore, they had no great urge to talk about their activities. During this time, the various religious denominations started to work together on a large scale. They shared their facilities and services, and many people had a deeper sense of God than you would find in normal times.

It was a time that forced everybody to take a stand and also to reflect on their values and purpose in life. I was blessed with an optimistic nature. However, that didn't mean that I did not have many moments of despair. With so much time on my hands and the extreme confinement, this could easily have lead to a much distorted view. In particular, I gave a lot of thought to my feelings about God, especially after my miraculous escape. I reduced my thinking to a simple philosophy. I felt that man had a limited mind and could not grasp the meaning of infinity. Science seems to assume a beginning and states that something cannot be created out of nothing. Yet, where did our universe come from? I reasoned that there is a power beyond our understanding that we call God. I found New Testament teachings to be both practical and to provide ideals to strive for. Love is the essential component of living your life. I felt that all the fights over and in the name of religion were man-made and in direct opposition to what the Bible tells us. This practical application of my beliefs has stayed with me all through my adult life and has served me very well. This belief in a non-denominational loving God helped me to fight my fears and sense of hopelessness and, as a matter of fact, prevented me from total collapse. I asked myself many times whether I was going insane and whether I was really as inferior as the Nazis tried to tell us. I questioned why I was not braver and why I was not a more active participant in the underground. My only explanation is that the circumstances were such that it never occurred to me that I should get involved. Maybe that was cowardice. I don't know.

Meanwhile, we listened to the BBC and a US radio station from Boston. The BBC consistently tried to communicate a straight-forward story while radio Boston had the Madison Avenue public relations approach. We were in the midst of the war until the last day in 1945. The last year of the war could truly be called the survival of the fittest. People dropped dead in the street from starvation. The Nazis became even more vicious and made constant raids of whole neighborhoods. The day and night firing of the V2's put us on edge all the time and some people had nervous breakdowns because of the extreme conditions. It was interesting to note that the British bombed the V2 installation almost every night, and later they bombed during daylight. However, they were never able to make a direct hit, and so their firing went on, destroying the neighborhood in the process.

One day, we heard a rumor that the German armies were on the run and that the Allies were negotiating a food drop for us. At that point in April 1945, the German regular army and some of the SS troops and Gestapo were starting to have some fear that they may lose the war. All of a sudden, there was some indication that they were starting to hide their atrocities and their reign of terror in order to save themselves. Therefore, they agreed to the food drop. It was to be done by allied planes flying low along a designated path and then, in our case, dropping the food on a nearby stadium field. The day came when we saw the British planes one by one flying the corridor and dropping the food on the stadium field. Then the Americans came. They didn't believe in flying in one by one. They came in a mass formation and dropped food everywhere. It was well-meant, but the population was so starved that, when they saw food hanging from trees, all around us a lot of fighting started as everybody wanted to get as much food as possible.

Then the day came that we heard a rumor that the Germans had surrendered, and it didn't take long to hear actual confirmation. It is hard to describe the reaction. It had taken so long that it was difficult to understand what it meant. This feeling is so deep that even now, when walking in the streets, I almost always feel how wonderful it is to walk the streets as a free man. My underground parents wanted to celebrate and, for that very purpose, they had kept a bottle of cognac that dated back to the days of Napoleon. Mrs. Holland didn't drink, so just the two of us were celebrating in this way. After many toasts and drinks, the doorbell rang. We suddenly realized that neither one of us was steady on his feet. Mrs. Holland was in the back of the apartment. I crawled on hands and knees to the front door and there was the landlady. She was surprised at my posture on the floor, but I was somehow able to explain to her that we were celebrating and were probably inebriated. When I then told her that I had lived in the apartment for more than two years, she couldn't believe it. She was a bit eccentric. However, we could have trusted her.

It was hard to believe that the war had finally ended. We had lived for so long in both physical and emotional pain that it would take a long time for the healing process to run its course and for us to get some balance in our lives. I said farewell to my saviors. I had a friend who somehow had obtained some of that exceptional commodity, gasoline, which was a very rare commodity indeed. Fuel disappeared very early in the war and, though you did see some cars with a big balloon on top filled with methane gas, you also saw cars with a horse pulling the vehicle. Eventually the main mode was bicycling or walking. The Germans, of course, had confiscated all the gas reserves. The underground also had blown up many gas tanks. They also changed all the road signs so that the German trucks would get lost or drive into each other. In Amsterdam, with the many canals, at night the underground pushed as many trucks as possible into the canals. They also changed the signs from left to right or vice versa so that, in the total blackout, the trucks would make wrong turns and thereby end up in the water.

I joined a friend and some other men and rode in the back of a truck from Scheveningen to Amsterdam. Since there were practically no civilian trucks and the Germans had left, when we passed through the towns and villages, people thought that we were part of the Orange Brigade, which was a military group of Dutchmen who had escaped to England during the war. Everybody was cheering us on, and it was a warm feeling to see the jubilant crowds all over. When the Canadian army arrived a few days later, I was in Amsterdam and saw them enter over one of the bridges. They had heavy army trucks, but the crowds swarmed all over the trucks and hugged the soldiers. It was an unforgettable sight, and I am sure the Canadians must have truly felt like war heroes.

I returned to my family, to my mother and brother. My mother had rented a furnished apartment in a nice part of Amsterdam. Our original home had been taken over by the Nazis and, although we saved some of our belongings, most of them were stolen. The owner of our apartment was a German woman with a daughter both of whom were as anti-Nazi as we were.

During the war, we had only one letter via Switzerland from my father in New York. I understand that the underground cooperated with the American FBI and smuggled correspondence to various families. We were also able to mail some letters to my father in the same fashion so that he knew that we were still alive. Now, we began receiving care packages from the US, and life started to slowly go back to normal. Whole parks and woods had disappeared. The tracks of the streetcars were not usable as people had taken out all the railroad ties. In many houses, furniture and whole sections of the house had disappeared, including stairways, as all this was used as firewood. Even with all of that, our joy of living was tremendous.

Shortly after the liberation, three officers from the Dutch Irene Brigade came to see us. One was my father's friend. He had promised my father that he would find us, and through the military communication system, informed my father. These officers had such a different attitude than what we were used to from the Germans. One was a colonel and the others had lower ranks. It was hard to distinguish the various ranks as they didn't even wear their insignia in contrast to the German army which had very strict rules. For example, a German officer could not walk side by side with a German soldier. The Dutch officers asked us lots of questions and also had some information about my father. They shared their supplies with us—even their chocolate. Later on, we had three Canadian officers stay with us. These Canadians had done some fierce fighting and had seen a lot of the cruelty that the Gestapo had inflicted on us.

Some people did start taking some revenge. Collaborators were taken from their homes by the underground forces or others and their hair was shaved off. Then, they were put on wagons and pulled through the neighborhoods where people could yell at them and throw things at them. In many of their homes, we found substantial supplies of food and coal and luxury items that they had stolen or confiscated from their fellow Dutch citizens.

We had volunteered to house children who were returning from concentration camps. One day, a Red Cross employee, accompanied by three children, rang the bell. One child was about ten years old and the others a lot younger. They huddled together, and the oldest really played the role of father and mother. They were totally estranged from normal human relations, and we had to be extremely careful and understand how void of any human feeling they were—other than their desire to cling to life. They had never slept in a bed, and we had to show them how to use the bed sheets. Most of the food they had never seen or tasted, and they were very suspicious of anything that was new to them. With lots of loving and patience, they started to unfreeze. I doubt whether any of these children could ever forget or learn to overcome the frightful experiences they had endured.

Sometime later, we housed a daughter of a friend of my aunt in Belgium. She had survived a concentration camp. She was in her twenties, a very attractive and bright young lady. I believe that she had lost her sister in the camp, but her spirit had survived and had probably made it possible for her to endure the concentration camp. I found it interesting that people who could relate to others and form bonds and have a belief in something apparently were more able to cope with the torture they had to endure. People without these attributes, even with a strong physique, often didn't make it. In general, it is my impression that women were much more tenacious than men and were a formidable force against the Nazi onslaught. My mother performed many heroic acts and helped to save many lives.

The girl, who I will call Sandy, went through a painful experience while living with us. One of the Canadians living in our house was not familiar with the history of her life. He started to date her. They both became very serious about each other. Then, one night, Sandy came home obviously extremely distraught and without our Canadian friend. My mother talked with her. That evening, he had commented to her that it was too bad that Hitler had not had enough time to kill all the Jews. She was in shock and told him that she was Jewish and had survived a concentration camp. He was totally dumbfounded and told her that she couldn't be Jewish because she was beautiful and wonderful to be with. She left him standing there and ran home. She was in hysterics because she really did love him, but now never wanted to see him or talk to him again. My mother wanted to try to repair the damage and talked to the Canadian officer. He was as depressed as she was. He told my mother that he grew up in a small town in Ontario, and it was common to make derogatory remarks about Jews. As none were living in the town, it was traditional, without much attention being given to the subject, to blame Jews for anything and everything. He had made the remark to Sandy without giving it any thought. He now understood how she must have felt and how utterly stupid it was just to follow the crowd and make these kinds of remarks. He wanted to do anything to repair the damage, and he tried very hard as he was really desperate to regain her respect and love. Unfortunately, the wounds were too deep for Sandy to be able to forgive him, and they never dated again.

Until my mother died, I had a standing disagreement with her about her attitude toward the German people. My argument was that, in all groups of people, there are good ones, bad ones, and many in-between. It is hard to explain how Hitler was able to convince so many Germans to follow his policies of hate and destruction. However, a possible reason could be the shortsighted settlement that the Allies made at the conclusion of World War I, which, in fact, led to the starvation of many Germans. Poverty, of course, often helps to bring out the worst in people. My mother did not accept that argument and would not buy anything made in Germany or deal with any Germans. The world cannot improve if we do not follow the basic rules of "love thy neighbor". There are, of course, a lot of people in Europe of my generation who agree with my mother.

During this time, I started to date a girl who had lost her brother a few days before the end of the war. It was a horrible story. Her brother had been very active in the underground and had been caught. The Gestapo took him home so that they could also interrogate the family. Only the mother was home at the time. For hours they questioned the mother and informed her that she had brought up her son in the wrong way because of which they should shoot him right in from of her. Then, they proceeded to do just that. The family was very prominent in Holland. Her father was a senior minister in the Dutch Reformed Church. The first time that I was invited for dinner, I was very nervous to meet the formidable father. When we started the dinner, there was no blessing said. During the dinner, the father all of a sudden turned toward me and said, "Jim, you may be surprised that I didn't say a prayer before dinner. I only say a prayer when I feel the need, as I don't want to be hypocritical about it". He was my kind of guy, and the relationship with the whole family grew warmer. When I went to the US, my girlfriend and her mother came and stayed with us. Unfortunately, it became clear that we were not a good match for marriage. However, we remained life-long friends.

After the war, everything was destroyed and there was little money to rebuild the whole society. One of the towns hardest hit was Rotterdam. The whole downtown had been flattened by the Luftwaffe to scare the Dutch into a quick surrender. The fires were so intense that, days after the bombing, one could not get within a mile of the city because of the heat. Everywhere, things were in a desperate shape.

In general, although we were still lacking many basic things, I remember the first post-war year as one happy string of events. We were one of the first to be able to talk to my father on a telephone connection between Amsterdam and New York. He had made all the arrangements for us to come to the US. It would be a good thing for my brother and me because, despite the need for rebuilding, there was very little chance in Holland for a job. Everything was destroyed, and there was little money to rebuild the whole society. We never questioned my father's decisions. My father had bought a nice house in Flushing, NY, which even had a separate basement apartment for my brother and me, so that we could have parties without disturbing our parents. Therefore, we went to the US embassy to petition for emigration. It took us a year to get the proper papers. The ambassador told us that congress had not voted enough money to do all the paperwork in a reasonable time. He actually felt that this was done deliberately to slow down the number of people that could emigrate.

My New Life In
The United States

When we finally heard that we would receive our emigration papers, we called our father. A week later, my father came home from his office and stretched out on the sofa before supper and never woke up. He was 55 years old and had died in his sleep from a stroke. In effect, I had lost my father at fifteen when the war broke out. My father's death was a heavy blow for all of us as we had survived the war and now had lost our father. My mother decided that she was not going to the States, but that we should follow my father's wishes. My brother was trying to get into medical school, and I was to salvage my father's business and liquidate the estate. We went to the ambassador who told us that, on such short notice, they couldn't complete our emigration papers. He would furnish my brother and me with an emergency visitor visa. He also counseled us about life in the US. The main advice I recall was that in the US you have to use elbow grease and fight for your rights.

I will never forget the day my brother and I left our home and took the streetcar to the station to get to the airport. This was 1946. My brother was 23 and I was 21, and we were totally inexperienced in worldly travel. We had our Sunday suits on and two brand new suitcases. Our first handicap was that the streetcar conductor would not let us on because we had too much baggage. However, when we explained that we might miss our plane to America, he relented. The plane was a propeller plane. We made a fuel stop in Scotland and in Newfoundland. It was our first flight and started with much excitement.

One of the passengers was a personal friend of Prince Bernhard. The prince, as a token of his friendship, was piloting a military plane and made circles around us. Our pilot was not to be outdone, so he tipped his wings to greet the Prince. We were quickly getting airsick from all this commotion.

When we stopped in Scotland, we had a little time to walk around and tried our English on a local Scot. We could not understand anything he said and were quite discouraged. We later found out that the Scottish brogue could really be called a separate language! Around twenty-four hours later, we arrived in New York at what was then called Idlewild Airport. It was June, and it turned out to be the hottest day on record with high and miserable humidity. Our suits were made of heavy woolen fabric. We couldn't understand how people could live in such heat. One passenger had on a fur coat. Although she was visibly suffering, she kept it on as it was an impressive coat.

We went through customs, which turned out to be a nasty experience. In those days, the immigration officers were not trained in civilized behavior and treated passengers like unwelcome nuisances. When the officer examined my suitcase, he moved his hands over the bottom lining and felt some uneven elevation. Before we knew what he was up to, he had taken a knife and ripped the lining from the bottom. Apparently the cardboard under the lining had doubled up. No apology, no recovery for the damage. Was this just a typical New Yorker's way to ignore the whole situation? He told us to move on. Welcome to the US!!

We went to our new home which was near the US World Fairgrounds. Inside, it was a very attractive home. Outside, our surroundings were like a cement city. However, in those days, the cement city was still surrounded by farms. The local A&P got all its produce from these local farms. I had a hard time getting used to the New York summer and was probably the best customer of the one and only movie house as it had air conditioning.

Some of the experiences of getting familiar with New York ways were amusing on hindsight. I had never seen a cafeteria like Horn & Hardart. One day, I went at lunch time to this place and followed the massive crowd along the display counters. I had picked up a tray and put it on the metal rail, but was so awed by all the foods on display, especially since only recently I had been starving to death, that, before I knew it, the servers had put all kinds of food on my tray. I ended up with some sandwiches, a couple of hot dishes and a number of deserts. When I got to the cashier, she looked at me and said, "Are you going to eat all this?" She was the first person to take time out to talk to me. I was so embarrassed that I said, "Of course!" I told her that in Holland, we were used to big meals. I could feel her stare at my back as I moved to a table.

The emergency visitor's visa that my brother and I had used to come to the US was valid for six months. We then had to go outside of the US and file our immigration papers. My father had hired a lawyer who specialized in immigration. Since my brother had already started his medical studies at Boston University, I volunteered to go alone to Mexico and check in with the US embassy. Once the papers were all right, my brother would join me, and therefore lose less time from his studies. In 1947, I flew to Mexico, again in a propeller type plane. We made a stop in Houston. Apparently one of the tailpipes had fallen off of one engine. We were told that we would have to stay overnight as they had to send for a tailpipe at another airport. We were taken to a hotel and were told to be ready to leave for the airport at 6:00 a.m. When we arrived at the airport the next morning, we were told that they had brought the wrong size tailpipe from the other airport. We finally left by mid-afternoon.

Meanwhile, some Mexican friends of my father were nice enough to meet me at the airport in Mexico City. They were waiting and waiting and, as usual, they never got a straight story as to when my plane would arrive. I finally arrived at 1:00 a.m. By then, the friends had gone home. I went to customs, and they told me to sit in a waiting room. I sat there for about two hours, and I had no idea why. I tried to make some inquiries and finally found out that the customs officer expected a little tip. Otherwise, they would make you wait. I then went to one of the customs officers, gave him a tip and sailed right through. Meanwhile, my friends had returned, and they took me to a hotel where I arrived at around 1:00 a.m.

While I was waiting to check in, an American came over and said, "Do you speak English?" I said yes, and he responded by cursing the Mexicans. He said that he was so relieved to be able to speak English with me that he invited me to do the town. I said that I was dead tired, but he talked me into an excursion to see the Mexican nightlife. In tropical countries, people usually stay up late as it is cooler then. It was an eye opener as, in those days; most Mexicans were so poor and desperate that a lot of young girls became prostitutes. They became addicted to a drink that contained wood alcohol. They knew that they didn't have long to live, but life was so desperate that they didn't care. I found it thoroughly disgusting for American visitors or others to take advantage of these girls. My new-found American friend was telling me all this and showed me some of the places where the prostitution took place.

During the evening, he asked me what I was doing in, as he described it, this God-forsaken country. I told him that, in the morning, I was going to the American Embassy to process my papers. He told me that he knew the Ambassador and, since he was not busy the next day, he volunteered to go with me and introduce me. The next morning I went with him and walked through a waiting room which was filled with Mexicans. He knocked on the secretary's door, and she asked if we had an appointment. He said no, but insisted that he didn't need an appointment as he was a very important VIP and the Ambassador knew him. She held her ground and the dialogue got more heated. I already had a vision of losing my chances of getting my emigration papers. I finally asked what I should do, and she said, "Just like the others, you come at 8:00 in the morning and wait your turn. She left and closed the door. My friend was raging. I thanked him for his help and said that I could handle it alone.

The next day I waited my turn for some four hours and was then let in by the secretary. I apologized and explained that I really didn't know that man at all. We then talked a bit, and she noted that I was from Holland. She asked where I had learnt English, and I explained that I had done so in school and afterwards had practiced with three Canadians who had lived in our house after the war. She wanted to know their names and the towns in Canada that they had come from. She happened to be from Canada herself. I told her and, miracle of miracles, one of the Canadians also came from her hometown, Hamilton, Ontario. She actually knew him and, as a matter of fact, they had been dating. She wanted to help me with my emigration papers and told me to come the next day to the side door and knock four times and she would let me in. She also promised to expedite the whole process. She kept her promise. She told me exactly what day my brother should come. When my brother arrived, he only had to stay overnight to have his immigration papers processed. We certainly had been lucky to have a friend at the embassy. It shows both the power of a secretary and the miracles that can happen when you deal with people in a respectful way. My mother called it "Vitamin C" where the "C" stands for "Contact." I found that to be so true. Many times it is not what you know but who you know.

During my stay in Mexico, I had two experiences that I will never forget. I love to walk, and one time I stopped and listened to a few street musicians. After a few renditions, the music stopped and a young girl went around collecting money from the listeners. I dropped ten pesos in her little box. She looked at me and then ran to a man who was apparently her father to show what I had given. Ten pesos was equivalent to around one dollar. She chatted with her father and then returned to me and handed me a small piece of soap. I said that I didn't want it as I thought she was trying to sell it to me. A Mexican standing next to me said, "You are insulting her. She offered the soap as a gesture of thankfulness that you had made such a generous gift." He said, "You had better leave quickly because Americans are always insulting us." I told him that my Spanish was not good enough to understand what was going on and to tell her that I deeply apologized.

The second experience happened to me when my father's friend invited me to his home for dinner. Before dinner, he gave me a tour of the plant that he owned. At the end of the tour, I asked him if I could ask one of the girls at the plant for a date. He said, "Of course!" I found the Mexican girls to be very pretty with a statuesque bearing that made them even more attractive. I asked one for a date and she said yes. I was not allowed to pick her up at her home, but had to meet her at a certain street. I got a taxi that evening, and she was waiting for me with her mother. Her mother looked me over carefully and held a conversation with me even though my Spanish was limited. She allowed the date to proceed. I took my date to a nice restaurant for dinner. It was my good luck that the waiter was from Holland. He told me that, if it were not for him, I would have burned my mouth and stomach as it was an authentic Mexican restaurant with lots of hot spices. My date didn't speak English, but somehow we had a conversation going. She was very graceful and had excellent manners. After dinner, I suggested that we go to a movie. Unfortunately, it was all in Spanish, and I didn't understand much while she was crying and laughing. After the movie, I took her back to the street where we had met, and she thanked me again and again. I had enjoyed it as well. It was obvious that she was not used to dating and this had been a royal treat, and she really appreciated being treated like that.

The next morning when I went to the plant again, the owner took me aside. He asked, "What have you done? All the girls are talking about the nice Yankee." I told the owner about our date and then said hello to the girl. She had a present for me–a tie, which must have cost her half a month's salary. When I talked to the owner again, he explained that I had not been invited to her home as they lived in a garage. They could not afford an apartment, and they were so embarrassed about it that they had decided to meet me in the street. I commented that her manners were equal to anyone brought up in upper class circumstances. He replied, "We Mexicans are very proud people. We may be poor, but we know our manners."

Once our immigration papers were in order, it was time to turn my attention to my father's business affairs. My only experience with the diamond trade came during the year after the war. My father arranged a six month's training period at a diamond factory in Amsterdam for my brother and me. A worker sat at a workbench which had an unbelievably fast rotating steel disk. The diamond polisher would cover the disk with an emulsion of oil and diamond dust. Only diamonds can cut or polish diamonds because of the hardness of the diamond. Workers would manipulate three different holders which worked like the pick up on a record player. The diamond would be set in an attached clamp in a certain position. Then, by feel, or in my case by miracle, the worker could change the diamond to another position. A full cut diamond has, I believe, 54 facets on it. Each facet has another facet on the side which runs symmetrically with the top facet. This makes the diamond brilliant as it totally reflects the sunlight. This task was for me a total ulcer-inducing operation because, if you didn't put the diamond correctly in the holder, it could cut through the whole steel disk in a split second and possibly kill somebody in the direct vicinity. The workmen were really artists and, of course, had been doing this work for many years. My other concern was that a diamond is valuable and, by mishandling it on the disk, you could lose a lot of money. It didn't take me long to decide that the diamond business was not for me, but I never had a chance to tell my father.

I believe that most people at a young age have no clear vision what they want to do with their life. In my case, I had not the slightest idea. It was assumed that I was to be groomed to become a CPA. The reason for this assumption was that my uncle had built the largest accounting firm in Belgium, and he had no children. My brother had already made it clear that he was destined to be a doctor. Unfortunately, my uncle died of a heart attack during the war. His partners had gradually assumed the leadership.

Therefore, after the war when we made plans to go to the US, things were up in the air. My brother went on to Boston University. I stayed with my widowed aunt in our new house in Flushing. My aunt was an unusual woman. She was extremely bright and was fluent in a number of languages. While her husband had built a large accounting firm in Belgium, she herself had, prior to that, climbed the ranks in a large insurance company to become the executive secretary to the president. In effect, she pretty well ran that company. After her husband had died, she joined my father and went to the US. With no children and nothing to do, she helped my father in his business in New York and also took care of the house. She was a marvel and an inspiration to all of us. She lived till 93 and never complained. She read the Sunday Times from top to bottom and was conversant in all the current topics. She had one saying that I use all the time. When somebody did something nasty to her she would say, "I just rise above it."

I tried to understand my father's business and, since my aunt had been his right hand helper and also kept the books, she helped me get a good idea about the business assets and liabilities. Since I really had no interest in the diamond business, my main objective was to liquidate the company. I found some people to help me since I had no idea about the value of the diamonds my father owned or how to go about selling them. However, there always seems to be someone who wants to take advantage of a situation. One person, who claimed to be a close friend of my father, said that he would do anything to help out of respect for my father. He did help, but for the wrong reason. In those days, getting good office space in Manhattan was impossible. His strategy was to gain my friendship, help to liquidate as fast as possible and then take over the office. In retrospect, I probably liquidated the business at a too low price as I had absolutely no experience and was in a new country still trying to sort things out for myself. We did salvage enough capital to support us and get a good start.

It didn't take long for my mother to change her mind and decide to come to the United States. She spoke enough English to get around, which was a complete eye opener for her, and she grew so fond of the US that you could not say a bad word about this country. My mother had lots of friends in Holland and loved to be with people. She made it known that our house was open to anybody who came from Holland and wanted a little time to get oriented. As a result, we had many people who stayed at our house, and we had a wonderful time as most of them were good people to be with.

Meanwhile, a friend of my parents who had escaped from Holland early in the war had been very successful establishing an import and export business. He offered me an apprentice job. I accepted and learned a lot in a hurry, but it was a typical New York job with tremendous time pressures. I took the subway from Flushing to Manhattan. I learned exactly the place to line up in the station in order to be within a group that jointly were pushed through the door and then found a few inches of space to stand. Fortunately, you couldn't fall as there were too many people crushed together. I was proud to have learned how to stand in the shaking subway car and calmly read the New York Times. The challenge was how to hold the newspaper so that you could easily turn the pages without hitting your neighbors. Meanwhile, my work hours became longer and longer. The owner was never very encouraging. However, his wife, who was also involved in the business, took pity on me and helped me through many difficult moments. However, the tension got worse. I was still coping with overcoming my war experiences. One day, I was sitting at my desk and started to cry uncontrollably. My cup runneth over, so to speak, and thank God it happened. I decided to quit and take some vacation time. My girlfriend and her mother had come from Holland to visit us. At that time, we were still planning to eventually marry.

During this break, I did a lot of thinking and realized that many young Americans had also lost a number of years in their lives and that, therefore, I was not too old to go back to school. I recognized that, as I grew up, I was always a follower and not a leader. My one and only brother, who was only two years older than I was, had assumed a leadership role at home. Since my father was not home much, my mother, probably subconsciously, relied on my brother to play, to some degree, the man of the house. I didn't do anything to change that status. Symbolic of this relationship, everyone called me "broertje," the Dutch word for "little brother" until, one day, when I was a teenager; my piano teacher aunt decreed that everybody had to call me by my name, Jim. What my aunt said was taken seriously. Later, when the war forced me to stand on my own feet under severe circumstances, I seemed to have adapted to that situation quite well.

COLLEGE YEARS

The challenge now was to try to enter a college. As an immigrant and not being an American GI, it was almost impossible at this late date in August 1947 to find a school. Fortunately, we had made many friends and, through one of them, I got an introduction to Mr. Goodner Gill, the Senior Vice President of Rider College in Trenton, New Jersey. When we arrived for our appointment, I found that the brochure of the college was a little misleading. The school was in downtown Trenton and did not have attractive buildings. To embellish the brochure, they had included the Post Office Building as the main campus building. Rider really was a business school with a touch of liberal arts. My mother accompanied me, and we met Mr. Gill. He looked and acted like Winston Churchill, including smoking a cigar. After the introductions, he looked straight at me and asked, "Are you a Republican or a Democrat?" I said that I was neither as I still was trying to find out what this country was all about. He felt that that was a good answer and told me so. After a bit of third degree questioning, he informed us that I would be accepted in the night school of the college. He explained that the college was bursting at the seams with students, but that it would add a new dimension to the school to have student from the Netherlands. My mother reacted immediately and told him that a son of hers would not go to night school, but only to day school. He told her that was impossible. My mother then came up with one of her many original ideas. She said, "Mr. Gill, you look like you enjoy food." He confirmed that he did. She continued and proposed that she would personally cook a Dutch apple pie for him and, if it was as good as she said, he had to find a way to get me into day school. He accepted the challenge; it was as good as advertised, and I was admitted to the day school.

Going to school at Rider College was one of the best things I ever did. The school spent most of its money on acquiring top notch professors and little on facilities and ambiance. I received a BS degree in accounting and felt that I had received a good education. I also learned a lot outside the classroom. Rider offered an accelerated program so that I could graduate in three years. In the beginning, it was difficult to talk with my fellow students as most were GIs who had their own language and certainly did not use the King's English that I had learned in Holland. I slowly absorbed the new language, but not without some embarrassing moments. I had been asked to be interviewed on the local radio station about my war experiences. When I referred to one person as a bastard, I got a mild kick under the table. Of course, in those days, language was more censored, and that word was absolutely taboo on radio while my GIs used it as a basic word in their vocabulary. The other mishap on the radio was that I didn't understand the sponsoring system and advertisements. I didn't know that the program that I was on was sponsored by a Broadway show called The Pajama Game with Eve Arden. The radio hostess had given me two tickets to the show and, when we returned to the air after the advertisement, she asked me how I liked the show. I said that it was fair. I got a dirty look, but didn't get the message. She then asked what Eve Arden was wearing. I said it was something like a nightgown. She interrupted and said, "You mean an evening gown?" I said, "They all look the same to me." That was the end of my radio career.

I lived in a college dormitory and, when I introduced myself to my Canadian roommate, he looked at me with a funny look. He said, "How did you get into this college?" I asked, "Why?" He explained that he lived in a small town and that nearby was a colony of Vanderpols who had settled in that area many years ago and had rarely married an outsider. As a result, they were all a little weird.

I had a good year as most of the subjects I had already learned in the Dutch high school. I made it onto the Dean's list without really trying. That permitted me to concentrate heavily on my social life. I had a car as, on weekends, I went home to Flushing to keep my mother company. I didn't realize that having a car was a status symbol with the girls. Soon enough, I was able to get dates. Having been underground for so long, I really had to catch up. One Sunday afternoon, I got a call from a girl who asked if she could get a ride from me back to Rider. Her father brought her over, and we started for Trenton. It was early December, and the weather changed to a real Northeaster snowstorm. We crawled along and finally arrived near midnight in Trenton. I dropped her off at a private home in Trenton and went to my dormitory. My roommate was half asleep. He asked how the weekend went. I told him that nothing special happened. Then, I opened my suitcase and immediately realized that it was my passenger's as her lingerie was on top. My roommate immediately woke up and wanted to know more. I explained, but I had a funny feeling that he didn't believe me. He then suggested that, if I were a gentleman, I should return her suitcase immediately. I got in the car. At first, it wouldn't start. Then, when I finally got it going, I realized that I didn't know the girl's last name or the exact address. I did find the street where I had dropped her off and decided to ring the bells at the homes that looked like the house where I had dropped her off. It was now about one thirty in the morning. I rang the bell at the first house and, after a little time, a man answered the door in a robe. I said, "Do you have a girl living here by the name of Ann?" At that point, the man got angry and yelled that he would call the police. However, I stuck to my guns and left for the next house. At the third house, I hit the jackpot as the girl answered the door. I apologized. She was nice and even said that I could have waited until the next day. The worst part of this experience was that my roommate couldn't wait to tell the school newspaper what had happened. The article was headlined "Vanderflynn and His Love Affairs."

My second year at Rider was still academically easy for me, so I continued my social activities. In Holland, I had been an avid soccer player, so I tried out for the varsity team. They had a number of good players. One had been in the Olympics. I made the team, but now a new learning experience was to begin–how to cope with the coach. First of all, I had no idea what a coach did and, secondly, I had joined primarily for the sport and not for having to win at any cost. Right away, the coach ordered me to run around the field a number of times in order to get in better condition. I felt that I was already in good condition. He told me to just do what I was told. I soon found out that being on the varsity team was business and hard work. I did have a good time as we played well-known schools. It also entitled me to join the sports fraternity. During the hazing process, I had to measure the bridge over the Delaware River with a carrot stick. Others had to do that too. I figured out that was a sham while others literally went to the bridge and measured. I waited until all had returned and turned in my calculation which was, of course, based on pure fiction. They accepted my figures. The other challenge took place in the winter when they dropped me off somewhere on a highway with no money. Cars would not stop but, when I saw a bus coming, I took my chances and stood in the middle of the road. The bus had to stop and, after some discussion with the driver, he gave me a ride back. When I became a member of the fraternity, a real challenge was learning how to play poker without losing too much. These games would go on throughout the night and into the following day. It was an endurance test.

As most of my fraternity brothers were GIs, many still had a hard time adjusting to college life. In my second year, I was elected to become the house manager, and then I really learned how to deal with my fellow students. The GIs, most of them financed under the GI Bill, had barely enough to live on. In an attempt to solve their money problems, they would give me a sad story that they had to support a sick mother or sister and, therefore, could not afford to pay room and board. It was often a convincing story which they had practiced in the army. I got wise to that and told the mailman to give me all the mail so they could open the government check in my presence. Another problem was the raiding of the refrigerator which had the food for the next meals. In desperation, I had a heavy chain put around the refrigerator and had the chain bolted to the wall. The next morning, I came down to the kitchen and saw that they had sawed the floor under the refrigerator. The refrigerator box had sunk to the basement where they could open the door.

The most challenging experience was when the fraternity decided that the woman who did the cooking had to be fired. She had a husband who was an alcoholic and came regularly with his cronies to sleep off their hangover on the front porch of the frat house. The frat was in a good neighborhood, and the neighbors had complained about this.

As the house manager, it was my job to tell her that she was fired. She was a formidable woman and, on the Saturday morning that I was to speak with her, all the war heroes and athletes had disappeared. I talked with her and at first she cried but, when I told her that this was a fraternity decision and that I could not change it, she started to scream and threaten me. Finally she left and soon my brothers returned. The following day, the husband and his cronies returned with crowbars and sticks. They were going to ransack the building. This was no problem to my fraternity brothers as this kind of fight was like war and, in no time, they had beaten up the intruders and chased them away.

The following year, 1950, I became the president of the fraternity. Every year, the fraternity did a good deed on campus. This time, we had picked a fellow student who had a hunchback and a serious inferiority complex. We decided to coach him in singing and sign him up as a contestant in the local theater contest. In this singing contest, the applause would be measured and the loudest applause would determine the winner. The first prize was a suit and one hundred dollars. The first setback was when the voice coach informed us that our candidate, affectionately called Mo, could not keep a tune as he was tone deaf. He also had a strong voice, but with a very shrill pitch. We decided that, regardless, we would go on. We asked everybody we knew to come to the performance and applaud for him no matter how bad it was. The disaster was the evening of the performance. There were two shows, and they had changed Mo's singing to the second show. We practically had to lock Mo up as he wanted to disappear from fear. Everybody stayed for the second show and, although Mo forgot the words and went off key and the accompanist quit and the MC was beside himself, Mo won. He got the prizes and regained his self confidence to such a degree that he insisted on singing at each party he attended.

Because of my participation in the soccer varsity team, I was automatically a member of The Skull and Sabre Society. It was supposed to be an honor. The problem was that each member was assigned to be a referee in the intramural games. Of all things, I was assigned to referee basketball, a game that I didn't know anything about. I studied the rules, but the game went so fast that I had no idea what was going on. I finally decided that the safest way to make decisions was to go along with the biggest guy. That created many errors, but it saved my neck.

My life at college was quite active. I played a lot of tennis. After the game, we would go to a drugstore where I ordered a banana split and a coke. In those days, I didn't worry about calories or cholesterol. I did a lot of dating and met a number of interesting girls. One girl, a very attractive and well-educated woman, was from South Africa. I promised to teach her how to skate. She brought a girlfriend with her. Most of the time, I had to hold both of them up. In so doing, I once lost my balance and broke my thumb–quite embarrassing for Mr. Macho! Later, I went steady with a professional model from New York who had a beautiful southern drawl. One day she told me that her former boyfriend, a wealthy socialite, had committed suicide because she had told him that she was no longer interested in him. I don't believe that I really grasped what had happened and how to deal with my girlfriend telling me this. I was so impressed that she was interested in me that nothing else counted. After dating her for more than a year, she finally told me that her mother was a widow and that she counted on her daughter to marry a rich man so the family could live a comfortable life. I told her that I was not rich and, in a short time, the romance ended. I had a very hard time overcoming the feeling of rejection.

My mother had told me right from the beginning that she didn't like or trust the girl. However, her reaction actually made it more of a challenge for me to continue the romance. After the romance had truly ended, my mother tried to introduce me to girls that she thought were suitable. It almost became a game. My mother's ideas of a nice girl and mine were irreconcilable, and she finally gave up the effort.

My last year at college, I shared an apartment with three other students and that worked very well. We each did our share of housekeeping to the best of our abilities. My cooking was terrible and fixing things was not my strong point, so I concentrated on cleaning and shopping. I found it very helpful to be able to study in a quiet environment. I still don't understand how students can concentrate with the radio blaring or with the television on.

During this time, the Dean of Women, a proud woman who let everybody know that she was related to the Rockefellers, elected me to become one of the three judges to select the beauty queen for the

Mayfair Dance, which was the big social event of the season. The dean ran her department with an iron fist. She had strict rules for the girls' dormitories. On weekdays, the girls had to be in at 11 p.m. and, on Saturday, at 1 a.m. Because of those rules and her elaborate spy system, it was an interesting challenge, when on a date, to see how we could beat the system. We had some success, but many failures. Therefore, I was surprised that she had chosen me to be a judge. Perhaps, this was my chance for revenge. She usually suggested to the committee who she preferred to be the queen. I suggested to my committee members that we ignore her advice and pick a girl who was not popular, and also not particularly attractive. When the dean became aware of this, she made life miserable for us. However, we stuck to our guns, and we won our case.

When it was time for my graduation, I went through a nerve racking experience at the graduation ceremony. A week before graduation, I was approached by the official in charge of the ceremonies. He asked if I could substitute for the person who was going to play the Warsaw Concerto at the graduation. I had continued my piano studies throughout my college years and, without really thinking it through, I said yes. When I began to study the concerto, I found it more difficult that I had thought and became quite anxious. However, my pride would not let me give up. The result was that I played most of the piece by knowing the melody and faking the accompaniment. Fortunately, enough people didn't know enough about music to know the difference between a fake and the real thing, so I squeaked through.

Looking back on my college years, I really learned about American life and gained a good preparation for my career. Rider College has done very well and is now recognized as a well-respected university.

Touring our New Country

After graduation, I began to look for a job. Luckily, I was able to find an interesting job through the efforts of my brother. While studying to become a doctor at Boston University, he lived extremely frugal as his studies were quite expensive. He gave his blood regularly to the Red Cross. The money they would pay him for doing this helped to defray his expenses. He lived in a very poor neighborhood and had very little social life. One day, he was waiting at a pier in Boston Harbor to meet a friend who was arriving from the Netherlands. While waiting, he met an older gentleman who was also waiting to meet the same person. They started talking, and the man invited my brother to his home. He proved to be a very wealthy wool merchant. The man was impressed with my brother and invited him regularly to his home for a meal. My brother told him about me and mentioned that I was looking for a job. He offered to talk to me.

I was interviewed by one of the two brothers who owned the company. The family was originally from the northern part of the Netherlands and had come to the US in the thirties. The company was one of the major importers of wool in the world and had large trading operations in the major wool centers in places like Australia, New Zealand and Argentina. The company had a plant in Holyoke, Massachusetts, for the purpose of combing the wool. They also still had an office in Holland. I was offered a job in accounting with the promise that I would be trained to succeed the treasurer of the company. As part of my compensation, I could live rent-free in a small apartment building on Commonwealth Avenue in Boston. In return, I was to be the superintendent of the building. It was really a lucky break to get this job before even starting my career.

Before starting my job, my mother and I traveled by car to Colorado to become more familiar with some of the beautiful places in our new country. We drove a number of days taking the so-called southern route at a leisurely pace and stopping at various locations. It was an eye-opener as we now really became aware of how big this country is, especially when you drive through the mid-west where you have these endless highways which, in those days, were not very crowded. I remember driving in Kansas and only seeing a few cars. Our first major resting spot was the Broadmore Hotel in Colorado Springs. It was a beautiful, well-maintained old hotel that had everything you could want in sports, entertainment, food and ambiance. I had never seen anything like it. The first night, when we entered the dining room, I was told that I had to wear a tie. I had no ties with me, so I went to the men's shop in the hotel. A husband and wife owned the store which was very expensive. I explained my dilemma and the wife, who had listened to my story, said, "Jim, I will lend you a tie." We got into a longer conversation, because she was very interested to hear about Holland as her college-aged daughter was traveling that summer in Europe. We had such a pleasant conversation that we made a promise to come back the next day and talk some more. We had a wonderful time during our stay at the Broadmore and became friends with the owners of the store. They apparently owned a number of stores and lived in Milwaukee. They insisted that, on the way back, we come and stay with them so they could show us Milwaukee. We didn't make definite plans to do so as, in Holland, you didn't respond so quickly to people you had just met.

After leaving the hotel, we headed out for a dude ranch in the mountains. We really had no good idea what a dude ranch was, but we were told that it would give us a real good idea what life in that part of the country was like. The journey took us longer than we thought it would, and it was getting dark. We were high in the mountains and had just passed a sign that said, "Proceed at Your Own Risk." My mother thought it would be wise to turn around and go back to a safer place.

The mountain road barely could accommodate two-way traffic and, on the right side, the mountain went straight up and, on the left side, it went straight down. My mother never lived it down that she offered to get out of the car to direct me in turning the car around. I accused her of being chicken, but I was really just as scared. Right then, a car approached. We stopped our turning around process and asked how far it was if we continued to the ranch. The occupants of the car said that it would take about ten minutes. We then followed them and arrived safely.

The dude ranch was an attractive wooden building, and the manager was extremely friendly. After a few days, we noticed that most of the guests were from Texas. This was a new experience for us. Unfortunately, none of them went out of their way to say hello or to be sociable. We asked the manager whether we had done something to offend them. He explained that, since we had a funny accent, they were watching us to determine if we were acceptable. He predicted that it would not take long before they would become friendly. Most of the guests knew each other as they came each year at the same time. Sure enough, before too long, one man started a conversation with us and, before we knew it, we were the main center of their interest. Their hospitality was unbelievable. They showed us around and treated us to dinner and shows.

They also insisted that we participate in horseback riding as that was what the dude ranch was all about. We had rarely been on a horse in Holland. They told us that the owner of the dude ranch was a famous horseman. He was in his early seventies and had last year married a twenty year old young lady and they had a little baby. We were curious to meet this famous biological miracle and did. The next morning, he hoisted us up onto a couple of well trained horses. Since we were using a western saddle, we didn't have to do much other than try to stay on top. He told us that the horses would know what to do, and he led the pack. We were on the horses for more than two hours, climbing all the time. We held on when the horses decided to jump over little streams. We finally reached a peak, and we were helped to dismount. The rancher explained that we were on top of Pike's Peak. The humorous part was that tourists had driven up to the spot in their car and were admiring us as the real Westerners. After lunch and some sightseeing, we were back on our horses for the journey down the mountain which turned out to be more frightening that going up. However, we made it, and the greatest miracle was that our rear ends had survived this venture without too much pain. We had a wonderful time at the ranch and many invitations to visit our new Texas friends which we unfortunately never did.

Later in the trip, we stayed a few days at Yellowstone Park and were awed by the beauty and marvels of the park. However, we were not used to the drastic change in temperature between day and night. One day, we were driving all day and complaining about the extraordinary heat. In the middle of the afternoon, we finally figured out what the problem was. The night before, we had gone somewhere and it was cold, so we turned the heater on in the car. We never turned it off until that next afternoon.

On our way back east, we decided to make a detour and say hello to our friends in Milwaukee. When we located their home, which proved to be a mansion on a lake, we rang the bell. A butler opened the door, and we told him who we were. The butler told us that we were expected. We had a wonderful time and then announced that we had better be on our way. They said, "You can't do that because the butler has already unloaded your car." They pressed us to stay for a few days so that we could see this part of the country. Their hospitality was overwhelming. An added bonus for me was that the lady thought that I would be a good young man for her daughter to meet. She asked if I could meet her daughter at the pier in New York upon her return from Europe and take her to the airport. I said that I would be delighted to do that. Unfortunately, I never met the daughter as she changed her plans and flew back to the United States.

Our next major stop was to see the Niagara Falls from the Canadian side. We crossed the Peace Bridge and stopped at Canadian customs. Before leaving the US, a sign on the bridge said that all you need to enter Canada is your driver's license. However, when we talked to the Canadian custom officer, he asked for our passports. He said that, because we were not born in the US, we needed to show our passports. We said that nobody had told us about this, and our passports were in New York. This happened on a Saturday afternoon, and this officer seemed to be fairly inexperienced. He said, "You are in a lot of trouble because you cannot enter Canada, and you cannot return to the US without a passport." My mother didn't take this very seriously and said, "Well, officer, if you can provide us with a tent, then we can camp on the bridge until you have straightened it out". He didn't think that comment was very funny and ordered us to follow him. He was going to call Washington for instructions as all of his superiors had gone home. He called and finally found somebody who told him to ask us questions about our emigration and, if our answers were satisfactory, he should escort us back to the US side and explain the situation. The officer then started to ask us some obscure questions that we couldn't answer. What is the size of the application form for US immigration? What was the color of the application form? Was your picture on the top right side or the left side of the form? In despair, he said that he had to call Washington for further instructions because what they had suggested was not working. After the usual wait, he got the same person. The Washington official started yelling at him and said, "You asked the dumbest questions. You are wasting two telephone calls on this. One final question: Do they look like murderers or gangsters?" The Canadian officer said, "No." The other voice screamed, "Then, don't waste my time and let them go!" We were then escorted back to our car where a guard was standing watch. My mother, who never gave up, whispered to the guard, "Do you know a way to see the falls from the Canadian side without going through all this trouble?" The guard said, "Lady, I had to stay here longer because of you. Please hurry up, or I will shoot."

Our last stop was Cape Cod. We had not made any reservations and arrived in the late afternoon in Hyannis. We tried several hotels and finally found a small hotel which seemed to cater to the elderly. We signed in and I got a complimentary ticket for a drink at the bar. It was just before dinner, and everybody was sitting on rocking chairs on the porch. While we were unpacking, my mother suggested that we should do something to liven up the place. I counseled against that as it usually meant trouble. However, after dinner we went into town, and my mother went into an ice cream store. She asked if they sold chocolate jimmies which they did. My mother then ordered two cartons of jimmies. I asked her what that was for and she said, "You will see." Now I was a little apprehensive. When we returned to the hotel, everybody had resumed their positions on the porch. My mother gave me one of the cartons of jimmies and said, "Follow me." She then started at the entrance of the porch and invited the first male guest to join her in a conga line. He could not refuse as she had already pulled him gently out of his rocker. She then went, "One Two Three Cha Cha Cha" and shook the carton. Before we knew it, she had everybody in the conga line, and we cha cha'd through the lobby and the kitchen and right into the bar. She announced that the first drink was on the house as she guessed that nobody had used their complimentary drink tickets. It became a real party, and later the manager thanked us because we had broken the stiffness of the guests, and they had never done so much business in the bar.

Our last experience on this memorable trip was going to a recently opened cinema in Hyannis one evening. The parking lot was huge, but they had not yet painted the individual parking spaces. We were with friends. The husband was a highly placed official with the United Nations. He was known as a practical joker. When we returned to the parking lot, it was a mess because of the lack of markings and no organized parking. The next thing I knew, our friend had found a small crate. He took it to the center of the lot and climbed on top of it. He then directed all the cars in such a way that eventually they were lined up in even rows facing the crate. He then left the crate, and we went to our car which was the only one not in a row, and we were able to leave unhindered. It was good that the next day we left Hyannis for home.

Starting Work at
Hart, Inc.–Boston

I started my job in Boston at Hart, Inc., a wool company on Summer Street across from South Station. This was in the fall of 1950, at which time Summer Street was the center of the wool trade. I met my new boss, the treasurer, who was in his late fifties. He was not an imposing man physically, but had a very powerful brain. He had a heavy German accent; with my Dutch accent, we made quite a pair. He was very friendly toward me and a good teacher. The office was rather modest with a small accounting staff and a number of salesmen and secretaries. One part of the office was used by the trading company and the other by the administration of the Holyoke plant. One owner brother managed the plant and the other the trading company.

I began to learn some facts about wool. Like any natural product, different types of wool had different characteristics, and therefore, it took years to become knowledgeable. A wool expert would know the difference in wool characteristics from different countries, from different ranches, from different types of sheep, different climates and different types of soil. It was really fascinating to see how quickly a pro could analyze a wool sample. The accounting was also fairly complicated as each wool lot had to be separately priced. We also had to be familiar with the financial documents, shipping and customs.

I progressed in coming up to speed quite well until the treasurer had a serious heart attack and was not able to return to work. The brothers talked to me separately and both confirmed that they had promised to train me to become the successor to the treasurer. However, they realized that I hadn't been there long enough to take over the job. They offered to bring in the financial man from their Buenos Aires office, which was the largest operation in the organization. He would stay for a year to help me, and then I had to assume the responsibilities of the treasurer. It was a very generous offer, but a high risk one because, if I could not handle the job, I would probably be terminated. I figured that this was a great opportunity and accepted the challenge. The treasurer from Argentina was excellent and also spoke good English. After a year, I felt comfortable enough to handle the job. The most difficult function was the accounting for wool futures contracts. It was mind boggling and, of course, a very risky business. However, because we had the wool experts in the business, the owners felt that they could outsmart the market. Over the long run, that proved to be wrong.

The wool trade had its own distinctions. Many old Bostonian families had made a lot of money, and they were a group with close personal bonds. They held many colorful parties. At a major affair of the wool trade, held in one of the better hotels in Boston, prizes were part of the proceedings. The day before, there had been a golf outing, and the winner was going to be awarded a fancy lawnmower. By the time they awarded the prize, the recipient had toasted many of his friends and was rather inebriated. He said that he wanted to try the mower and, before we knew it, he was mowing the plush Persian rug in the banquet hall. That must have been an expensive mistake!

Many wool firms had hospitality rooms, and I was in charge of ours. Late that same evening, a well dressed gentleman came into the room and asked if he could borrow a few bottles of whiskey as his company had run short. Since there was a kind of brotherhood mentality in the trade, I didn't feel any problem with giving him a few bottles. Little did I know that the man had a truck outside and had gone to the various hospitality rooms with the same story and had assembled a good inventory of liquor.

Another story in the trade involved two well-known wool merchants who regularly pulled practical jokes on each other. One time, one of them ordered a hearse and told the driver that his best friend had died. To help the widow, he was to pick up the body and deliver it to the funeral home. The driver went to the home of the other merchant and created an unforgettable scene when he told the wife that he had come to pick up the body of her deceased husband.

I was well paid, especially at my young age, but I found that there was a major problem with my job. The two brothers didn't like each other and were completely different in personality. In my job as treasurer, I had to confer with them almost on a daily basis. One was a born salesman and very outgoing. The other was a man who was difficult to deal with. They both were very rich and had developed some of the peculiarities of the rich. The more difficult brother invited me for lunch one day and drove me in his big limousine to the other side of Boston to a Tom McAnn shoe store. He told me that he only kept one pair of shoes. He liked the salesman at that store and bought a new pair of shoes from the salesman every three months. If you counted the long ride and the expensive lunch he treated me to, the shoe shopping excursion was not inexpensive. Another time, he asked if I could keep him company on a trip to Ithaca to visit his son who was a student at Cornell. When we arrived at the hotel, there was no parking space as it was a big weekend. He told me to move one of the signs in front of the hotel that said "No parking between signs." As he insisted, I did as I was told. Unfortunately, in the middle of the act, a policeman showed up and gave me a stern warning that I could not do that. I got back in the car. My boss said, "Let us drive around the block because the policeman will continue his beat, and then we can move the sign." He may have thought that this was quite clever, but the plan didn't work. He got an expensive ticket and subsequently asked his lawyer to fight it. His main complaint was that the city should be more hospitable toward its visitors. Between the lawyer and the ticket, the whole affair cost him a lot more than if he had found a garage.

The major problem that I had was that I became more and more a referee between the two brothers. If one claimed that a certain wool lot should be accounted for in the plant, the other would say that it should be booked in the warehouse of the trading company. It was a no win situation as each told me that, if I did not follow his orders, I was fired.

At Christmas time, the secretary of one brother typed greetings and wishes on beautiful Christmas cards. She told me that she had to do that each year, including sending one to herself. It just never occurred to the man that that was not exactly in the Christmas spirit.

My additional job as superintendent of the apartment house also led to some interesting experiences. There were three apartments, and each held a family which was a story in itself. On the first floor was a gentleman in his seventies who came from a wealthy family in the shoe business. He told me that, when he graduated from Harvard, he told his father, who was the president of the shoe company that he had decided not to make a career in the business. The father felt that the son would be a disaster for the business, and was so relieved with that decision that he gave him a life's income. The son went back to school, mastered three languages and then traveled extensively to see the world. Subsequently, he went to the American Express company and proposed that he could take a group on a guided tour several times a year. In return, he didn't require a salary, but merely the covering of his travel expenses. They accepted his offer. He kept up his reading in four languages and was a pleasure to converse with. He had many stories to tell. He never got married. He said that he had decided that if he would marry, it had to be a brunette, but he always fell in love with a blonde or a redhead.

When he was in his sixties, he didn't feel so well. He went to a doctor who told him to cut out the smoking and heavy drinking. He also should move to a downstairs apartment or move to a building with an elevator. At the time, he was living on the fourth floor. He said that he followed the doctor's orders and felt miserable. He then found another doctor who smoked and drank. The doctor told him that the cure was worse than the disease and told him to go back to his old lifestyle. It seemed like good advice. Much later on in his eighties, he moved to Italy and was still going strong.

During my acquaintance with him, he moved to an apartment on Marlborough Street where the owner only rented to people who studied the piano. I moved there as well as I continued with my piano studies. The arrangement was practical as none of the tenants could complain about the noise. My friend treated me royally and was great fun and interesting to be with. He drank a lot, but never got drunk other than dozing off.

His language was exquisite. One day he told me, all excited, that he had a new student that he was going to tutor in English. She was a Swedish airline hostess, and the way he described her was that she was a heaven-sent beauty. His description was so imaginative that I was dying to meet this rare specimen. Unfortunately, when I did meet her, I found that his language had far over-shadowed reality.

One day, he took me to show me the dormitory where he had lived during his Harvard days. He said that everything was very elegant. They had butlers and housekeepers. When, after considerable knocking on the door of his former abode, a student opened the door; he was half dressed and unshaven. One peek through the doorway showed on unkempt dump. My friend was in total shock and turned around and quickly left, absolutely speechless. When I worked later on for various colleges, it was always a concern of the administration how to explain to the alumni that most students today seem to be totally uninterested in keeping their rooms in some presentable state.

During these bachelor days, I met a girl who I was seriously dating. She invited me to her home in Chestnut Hill. The parents seemed to be very nice. However, the mother asked too many questions. That summer, they invited me to visit them at a very exclusive hotel on Cape Cod. When I arrived, the mother greeted me and told me that it was better if I didn't see her daughter anymore. She gave me some vague reasons centering on incompatibility. I was disappointed. The next day, I saw a friend and told him what happened. He said, "I know this family. They are known to be social climbers and live way above their income to make it possible for their daughter to meet the right people." He said that this would be a wonderful time to teach them a lesson as they probably turned me down because I was not wealthy enough to be considered. He said that his niece had a coming out party that was going to be the social event of the season. She had not been able to find a suitable escort. He could talk to his sister about me and tell her that I would be happy to be the escort. He also would insist on inviting the parents and daughter who had turned me down as a suitor. They would sit at the worst table, while I would sit at the head table. I liked the idea, but questioned whether they would come. He said, "Of course they will come. It shows true status to be invited to this party". The scheme worked out beautifully. I will never forget the looks of the family when they saw me at the head table.

Meanwhile, I adjusted to my new lifestyle. I even tried my hand at cooking. That proved to be too much of a challenge as one pan after the other had to be thrown away. I seemed to burn most of my meals. I found the solution by befriending a fellow bachelor. He was an engineer with Phillips in the Netherlands and had accepted a job with Raytheon in Boston. He had developed a listing of clubs and churches that, on certain nights, furnished dinners as a social occasion for non-members. I joined him, and we had most of our dinner problems solved. He also took me to Cranmore Mountain, as he was an avid skier and insisted that I should learn to ski. We made the trip, and I rented the necessary equipment. We took the lift to the top, and he showed me how to put on my skis. He left me with the advice that the best way to learn was by doing. I looked down the mountain and had a struggle between my pride and my common sense. My pride of course won. My solution was to zig zag down the slope because on both sides were trees which could stop me. It was an unforgettable experience. In the middle of the course, a beautiful, young lady had fallen and couldn't get up. I was just getting close, and she begged me to stop and help her. I couldn't stop, but was able to tell her that, at the next tree stop, I would turn around and come to her rescue. I didn't realize that it is dangerous to take your skies off and walk to the rescue. At the end of this adventure, I went straight to the Schneider Ski School and signed up for lessons.

Another priority was to find a good piano teacher, as I wanted to continue my studies. None of my friends could suggest a good teacher, so I decided to go to Copley Square and look around for music schools. This didn't produce any results. So, I decided to talk to the local pharmacist in Copley Square, as he probably would know a lot of people. He said that there was a very outstanding teacher right upstairs. His name was Julius Chaloff. After a considerable wait, Mr. Chaloff, formally dressed in a dark blue suit with gold framed glasses and a rather severe teacher's look on his face, greeted me. He asked who referred me to his studio. I told him the pharmacist, and that didn't impress him. He asked, "Are you a professional pianist or an amateur?" I told him that I was a serious amateur. He explained that he didn't teach amateurs as they do not work hard enough. However, after considerable discussion, he finally agreed to take me on a trial basis provided that I would practice at least two hours a day. I was willing to do that. Mr. Chaloff turned out to be an amazing man. Once you were under his wings, he helped in every way that he could. His lessons were always over an hour as he wanted to be satisfied that I understood what he had taught. Each piece of music had to be played exactly to his satisfaction. He had the entire basic classic piano repertoire in his head. He could recite what the notes were in any given measure of a piece of music. He had an unusual theory about how to practice. He felt that our brains were similar to computers in that, once the notes were clearly stored in the brain's memory, you would not forget them. The way to store the notes securely in memory was to study the notes so slowly that, between each note, you waited long enough that your ear could not tell you where to go next, but your brain would guide you to the next note. This was very nerve wracking but, when I finally mastered the technique, it worked. My piano skills, both popular and classical, opened many doors for me and enhanced my life.

In the year that I got my first annual bonus of $1900, I decided to buy my first car. I went to a Ford dealer, and an elderly man approached me. I told him that I had $1900 with which I wanted to buy a car. He smiled and said, "You were obviously not brought up in the US as you should never tell a car salesman how much money you have to spend. However, you are lucky, because I am an honest man and will give you a good deal". I ended up with a one year old blue hardtop Oldsmobile model 98. It was fully equipped, and was the best second hand car I ever bought.

I went regularly to New York to visit my mother on weekends. She had accumulated a large circle of friends and was starting to forget all the pain of the war. She started to date and was very much in demand. My mother was dating a widower from Brussels who came regularly to New York to visit his married daughter. He also had various businesses to attend to in the city. After a year of dating, he asked my mother to marry him and come with him to live in Brussels. My mother liked it so much in the States that she was not ready to make a quick decision. Her emotions went back and forth until finally the decision was made that she would marry him with the proviso that, a couple of months each year, she would come and stay in the US. With this arrangement in place, they were happily married for seventeen years.

I didn't see much of my brother as he was very busy with his studies.

He was dating a girl from Holland. One time, when she came with her father on a business trip to the US, we had arranged that my brother and his girlfriend would meet up with me and a girl that I knew from my high school days. We planned to go to Manhattan to a famous nightclub. Before we left, I drove my mother to a theatre. On my way back home, I got a flat tire, and it began to snow. I proposed that we not go all the way to Manhattan, but rather stay at our home in Flushing. I suggested that we play a game. I had been accused of being a sissy when it came to drinking. To once and for all disprove this, I said that I was willing to out-drink my friend from Holland. We would both drink whisky and, after each drink, we would have to stand on one leg and tell a funny story. My brother and his girlfriend were to be the judges. As I was making a fool of myself, my brother and his friend had a unique chance to discuss their relationship, which would not have been possible, had we gone to the nightclub. They had plenty of time, as it turned out, because it apparently took a long time for me to complete the process of making a complete fool of myself. I ended up crawling on my hands and knees up to my bed.

Early the next morning, my brother woke me up and said that, after talking it over, he and his girlfriend had decided to become officially engaged. With my head spinning, I made the supreme sacrifice and participated in a Champaign toast. His bride to be was an exceptionally fine lady and now, after more than forty years of marriage, it is one of the best marriages I have ever seen.

One weekend, I signed up at a tennis club. As I was sitting on a bench resting from a game, a beautiful girl named Dorothy approached me in a rather hesitant way and sat down. We made some general remarks and started to converse. She explained that she was an airline hostess with TWA and lived right next to the tennis club. She really wanted to play tennis and decided to just walk in and see if someone would play tennis with her. I, of course, came to the rescue. This developed into serious dating and even my mother gave tacit approval.

After a year of dating, we also decided to get married. Dorothy came from a small family near Tuxedo Park in New Jersey. Her mother was a widow. We decided on a very modest wedding and were married in New York in "The Little Church Around the Corner" on East 29th Street. Because my mother-in-law insisted on paying for the social event, we invited only the immediate family for a lunch reception at a hotel in New York. The previous night, my stepfather treated my friends and me to a fancy dinner at the Brussels, one of the top places in New York. During the dinner, two business friends from Brussels showed up, and he invited them to join us. Then, he invited them to join us for the wedding. This was a problem, because we had excluded many friends of long standing from the reception; however, I didn't want to say at the dinner that he shouldn't invite them. The result was that these best friends of my mother and father dating back to Amsterdam and now in New York were so insulted, that they never wanted to talk to us again. I told my mother that they were not really friends to react in this way. However, my mother was very hurt by this outcome.

Dorothy and I settled into my 4th floor Marlborough Street apartment. I had earned enough to have some nice furniture and even a beautiful baby grand piano. Dorothy changed her job with TWA from hostess to travel agent. We were quite busy with our jobs, especially since Dorothy had to work many nights and weekends. We had the advantage of getting free travel, and we spent our honeymoon in Bermuda. We almost had our first test of a good marriage as there was only one seat on the plane, and we couldn't reserve seats under the free passage arrangement. Fortunately, there was one cancellation, and we made it together to Bermuda.

After one year of marriage, we had our first baby. While I was waiting in the waiting room of the hospital, I saw the assistant doctor and the nurse coming into the room. They didn't see me, but I overheard the doctor say to the nurse, "Well, he screwed it up again!" We had chosen a famous obstetrician in his seventies for the delivery. Apparently he had lost his touch, and shortly thereafter retired. When I saw our baby, I noticed that her forehead was a flaming red color, and the sides of her head were compressed. When we took her to our pediatrician, he said not to worry. She would grow out of it. He explained that it had not been an easy delivery, and the doctor had pushed the forceps very hard. However, from early on, we had serious trouble with her. Feeding was a problem and her sleeping was very irregular. After some years of trying, we took the advice of my brother and urged the pediatrician to have a more thorough look at our daughter. He continued to insist that we shouldn't worry. However, the behavior didn't improve and was a drain on both of us. We didn't have a normal night's sleep for years. When we discovered that she would sleep when riding in a car, I would take her and drive her around in the evening. In the crib, she would also rock fiercely with her whole body and bang her head against the headboard. It was amazing that she survived. Dorothy had given up her job with TWA as taking care of our baby required full-time attention. However, no matter what we tried, her condition was never to improve.

COOPERS AND
LYBRAND–BOSTON

During this time, I had more and more reservations about staying with Hart, Inc. as the two brothers continued to fight relentlessly. I had written to my mother that I had decided to change jobs. She was just ready to come over to the states by ship. At her table was a partner of Coopers and Lybrand, a large public accounting firm. My mother described me in such glowing terms that he said, "I will talk to your son as I have never heard of such a perfect being". My mother told me about the conversation, and I responded that, with her exaggeration, he had just had a good time listening to her, but would probably not call me. However, he did call and, after some interviews, I was hired. This was quite a coup for me because, in those days, they hired mostly Harvard and other Ivy League school graduates. The job meant that I had to take a severe cut in salary and had to study to get my CPA certification. This was not easy as it required a lot of study to master the material, and this was complicated further by the situation at home. At this time, we had moved to an apartment in Hancock Village in Boston. My salary was clearly insufficient for our needs. To address this problem, I started a tax and accounting service at night. I was able to find some small companies and some individuals as clients and did very well with this. However, I was a little optimistic that my study for the CPA exam could be passed simply by taking a preparatory class at Bentley College. I failed the test. Then, I took a La Salle correspondence course and tried again. This time I passed all the subjects except law.

I received credit for the subjects passed and was allowed to retake the law exam–this time in San Francisco where I had an audit job. I almost missed the exam altogether, because I was sent to the wrong Masonic temple. However, I finally found the correct location and passed the exam to my great relief.

I have never regretted making the job change. I enjoyed my new career very much. An accounting firm devotes a lot of time and resources to train their professionals in all aspects of the financial world. Because of the great variety of clients, you get unique, practical experience. The Boston office was the second largest after New York, and yet there was a sort of family spirit. The competition between us was real, but we were competitive in a constructive way. Nevertheless, my first audit provided a shaky start. I showed up early at a factory in Charlestown which manufactured all types of screws. Since I was there early, the front door was locked. A woman, who introduced herself as the office manager, told me that she had the key to the front door, but had forgotten the key to her office. She asked if I was willing to climb over the partition and open her door from the inside; I agreed. She decided to go to the Ladies Room while I was accomplishing this. Just as I had raised myself to the top, my supervisor walked in and wondered what I was doing. I jokingly said that I was performing a public relations service.

As an auditor, my first task was to check the printout of the inventory to see that the printout conformed to data on the original inventory cards. The first card didn't check out, the second one also didn't and, in short, none of them did. I got nervous, and thought that I must have made a stupid mistake. However, I finally brought it to the attention of the supervisor. He came to the same conclusion. He said that it would be disturbing to bring this to the attention of the treasurer as he had absolutely no use for auditors. Nevertheless, he went to his office. I could hear the man yelling at my boss that we were wasting his time, and that he would now have to straighten out our stupidities. We didn't hear anything from the man for a few days, but he finally had to admit that he had made a mistake and had given us the inventory cards of the year before.

As I continued with the firm, I began to learn about the inner workings of our Boston office. The partners were considered as close to God as our imaginations could conceive. There was very little communication between partners and employees. The dress code was very strict. There were no female auditors. I also noticed that the workforce was basically the Old Boys Network – manned mostly by Harvard or Ivy League graduates. The senior partner took new employees on a walk through the various departments. As part of this tour, he introduced us to the woman in charge of the library and the audit files. He emphasized that there were strict rules that we should adhere to. In particular, the audit files were confidential and needed tight control. He then asked the woman in charge to explain the rules. She responded that she agreed 100% with the senior partner but that he should practice what he preached. Apparently, he was the worst rules offender. The senior partner just shrugged his shoulders. She had been there longer than anyone else and was not somebody to argue with. I found many times in my career that official titles did not always indicate who was running the show.

After I became a CPA, I was promoted to supervisor. One of my new assignments was to do an audit of a Brooks Brothers store. We did an extensive inventory audit and, when I finished writing up my findings, I got up and, as I did so, a button on my jacket hooked into the middle drawer and tore my jacket. The manager was in the room and said that he would get the tailor to fix it. When the tailor saw the tear, he said that it could never be properly fixed. The manager then offered to let me pick out a brand new suit as I could not leave the store with a torn one. I had to do some quick thinking as we had a very strict code not to accept bribes from a client. However, this was an accident and the suits were so appealing that I decided to pick out a nice suit and worry about the ethics later on. However, when I got home I did start to worry about what I had done and had a sleepless night. The next day I felt compelled to see the senior partner and explain what had happened and take the consequences. He was willing to see me. When I entered the inner sanctum, he told me to sit down but didn't even look up from his desk. After sitting there awhile, I had visions of the end of my career and began to get very nervous. He finally looked up, stared at me with a penetrating look and said, "What can I do for you?" I told him what had happened and asked what I should do. A painful silence ensued and then he said, "Jim, if you ask me a foolish question, I have to give a foolish answer. I don't like to do that so please leave." I walked out and had no clue whether I was okay or if I had been fired. Since nothing further was ever communicated, I concluded that I was still on the pay role. Apparently, word got around. Our office manager, who was always well informed, told the story to everybody. All of a sudden, the Brooks Brothers audit became so popular that I never got back on it. My suit was a wonderful suit and I enjoyed it for many years.

Once a year, we had a primarily social retreat. The firm outdid itself to make sure that everybody enjoyed the events. The retreats were done in different styles at different resort hotels. They furthered the camaraderie of the work force and I will always have good memories of those days. One of my colleagues had just returned from Navy duty and his reports were full of Navy slang. He would write that he had gone to the "third deck" to take inventory and that everything was "ship shape." It took awhile to change his ways.

The partner who had hired me was almost like a father to me. He was a wonderful man – very bright and very caring. Unfortunately, he had a drinking problem which he blamed on the firm. He felt that they had trained him in all the technical aspects of the firm but had never prepared him for the human aspect of the role of partner. As a partner, you had to deal with personnel problems and with clients of all types. In addition, the partner had the pressure of producing his own share of the fees. When I reached the senior levels of management, I saw the cruelty and the real and perceived pressures that can kill many a good person.

I never regretted that I made the move from a senior position at Hart, Inc. to an entry level position at Lybrand. I think that anyone who wants a business career receives an incomparable experience practicing public accounting. It sharpens your analytical skills, gives you a broad picture of a great variety of businesses, allows you the opportunity to deal with a cross section of the hierarchy, and provides a strong academic program to help with the intricacies of accounting and finance. During my relatively short stay in the Boston office, I was involved in auditing major universities, banks and manufacturing companies large and small. In between, I studied for my CPA exam and attended the Lybrand courses. It was a very rewarding experience.

The other bonus I received, though I was not fully aware of it at the time, was that Lybrand consistently hired the top students from the top colleges. I, of course, was an exception but it created an environment and a challenge to do as well as your peers. The standards were very high and, fortunately, the code of ethics for CPAs was strictly enforced. It resulted in a very positive experience that helped me throughout my career.

COOPERS AND
LYBRAND–PITTSBURGH

One day, I was called in by the senior partner who offered me a transfer to their office in Pittsburgh. One of their key clients was Alcoa. Alcoa had just signed a large contract with the government of Suriname in South America. Suriname used to be a colony of the Netherlands and was still heavily subsidized by the Dutch. Alcoa wanted someone who could speak Dutch to facilitate their dealings with the Suriname government. Who says that languages are not important? It meant a promotion for me as well as a one of a kind experience.

In 1958, when my family moved to a suburb of Pittsburgh, I immediately noticed how friendly the people were. When we were looking for a house, there was a particular home in Mt. Lebanon that I wanted to see again. I knew which bus to take, but couldn't remember exactly where to get off. I asked the bus driver and he said, "Well, I'm not too busy so I will detour the bus and drop you off in front of the house." None of the few passengers on board seemed to mind. Our moving was complicated. Because of our oldest daughter Nancy's emotional and mental problems, we had to make special arrangements for her. She was in a good residential home in Boston and now we had to find a new place for her in Pittsburgh. A Catholic institution, Clelian Heights, run by nuns, had an opening, and it was not a requirement that the family be Catholic. We moved Nancy, and she received excellent care.

I started my orientation at the Pittsburgh Lybrand office. The senior partner was a brilliant man. He was fair, but stern. His credo was: "If you can express something with one word, don't use two!" One exercise that I had to participate in for an entire week was to take legal briefs and reduce the text from three pages to one. At the same time, I was directed to improve the language so that an ordinary citizen could understand it. I struggled, but finally met with his approval. I was promoted to a senior position and had to take on a management position in the Alcoa audit at the same time as I was preparing for my assignment in Suriname.

There are basically two ways to manage other people—through compassion or fear. Management puts a stamp on a company and, as an auditor; I could recognize fairly quickly the type of operation I was dealing with. Alcoa fell more in the compassionate category as demonstrated by a low turnover of personnel and good, but average salaries. Companies who used high pressure and fear tactics usually had high turnover and high wages. My audits of Alcoa included visits to various plants such as Massena in New York and Davenport in Iowa. These plants were huge, and the equipment was very impressive. As an auditor, you dealt mostly with management. I made good friends. One plant manager had a weekly poker party and invited me to join. I didn't know too much about poker and paid more than my dues to learn the game. Another plant manager became a really close friend. One day, he called me into his office. He had received a call from headquarters in which they had offered him a big promotion and a move to the corporate office in Pittsburgh. This would give him a chance to climb the corporate ladder. His problem was that he liked where he lived and so did his family. He made an adequate salary that satisfied the needs of his family. He asked me for advice. I told him that he had already answered his own questions because of the way he explained the situation to me. The way that he phrased his questions to me showed that he wanted me to agree with him that he should stay in his current job.

Alcoa was very involved in automating their plants and started to use computers more and more. This was before the transistor. In the late fifties when the Univac computer was one of the more popular computers, computers were often down because a great number of their tubes always malfunctioned. The computer also needed a tremendous amount of air conditioning. If a thunderstorm was forecast, the machines had to be shut down because, without power and air conditioning, the heat inside the computer would damage the tubes, and the wiring could easily cause a fire. I ran into interesting auditing problems because of automation. One plant had their payroll on the computer and had a mysterious problem with disappearing payroll files. After a lot of probing, we found that the previous payroll manager had quit in anger and had not informed the new manager about the details of the payroll computer program. Inadvertently, the new manager had used a code which, in the existing program, was the code for dropping an individual from the payroll. As this was a very confidential code, only the old manager had been familiar with the instruction.

On the other hand, a consolidated computerized payroll, when operated properly, could eliminate some of the old problems with manual payrolls. One large client had two large plants within 20 miles of each other. I did a payroll audit in the first plant, and then moved to the second. I noticed in the second plant an unusual name on the payroll list, and I vaguely remembered that I had seen the same name in the first plant. I asked if there were brothers, one working in each plant. It turned out that the first plant had hired a truck driver some twenty years ago to transport materials between the two plants. Without consulting each other, the second plant had also looked for a truck driver for the same purpose. The man was a highly regarded employee, except that he had never said anything about his dual enrollment. He ended up getting double salary and overtime payments. The management was so embarrassed that they quietly retired the man.

I had learned a lot about Alcoa and was ready to help in the Suriname venture. Suriname is very important to the aluminum industry as it is a major source for bauxite which is the key ingredient in aluminum. Bauxite is transformed into alumina, which in turn is made into aluminum. Large quantities of electricity are required for this process. Alcoa had made an agreement with the Suriname government to dam the Suriname River in order to build a lake, which would provide the water for a big power station. They also wanted to build an alumina smelter. On my first trip, I found that my Dutch was totally unnecessary as all government employees spoke good English, and the natives spoke neither English nor Dutch. Alcoa planned to hire around twenty thousand natives and teach them the necessary skills for their tasks. The natives wore loin cloths, lived in the tropical jungles, were basically hunters, and had a basic Stone Age culture. They often had fire dances on Saturday nights, at which time there was a contest to see who could keep his naked foot in the fire the longest. The winner would automatically become the chief of the tribe. My challenge was to help Alcoa persuade these tribesmen to work for them. It soon became clear that Alcoa looked to me to find ways to make this happen. Obviously, there were no books written on the subject. Alcoa had a good team of people. After a lot of attempts, we were able to get the natives to work. I believe that they did so mostly out of curiosity. We found that some learned very quickly, even mastering the art of handling large bulldozers. Those who had a good feel for rhythm seemed to learn easily. However, the ones who didn't have that natural talent wrecked the machines very quickly. The agreement with the government was that the workers would get cash payment each week. I was involved in devising ways to provide payment. These people had never seen or used money before. They spoke a language that we didn't know. We finally devised a plan in which each man got a tattoo with his name. On pay day, we would repeat their name so that they got used to the sound. We also took pictures of each one and wrote their names on them so we could more easily identify them. Since they had never had any money, there was nowhere in their village they could spend it. However, the earnings were not the real motivation for them to work. It was rather that they liked the excitement of working with the equipment and the challenge of doing something new. Nevertheless, it didn't take too long before a small group of workers had found their way to Paramaribo, the main city in Suriname, where they discovered that money could buy things. The first possessions many bought were outboard motors that could attach to their canoes. It soon became a status symbol to come to work from the jungle on the Suriname River using a canoe with an outboard motor.

For a considerable time, we continued to have a problem having the men work on a regular basis. The old lifestyle of hunting and living off the jungle was more appealing to them than working regular hours for pay. This went on for at least a year, until one of the natives approached us and, in understandable English, told us that he had a proposal. He was aware of the absenteeism and proposed that a camp be set up where the workmen would reside during the week. He would feed them and make sure that they would not disappear. He explained that he had gone to Paramaribo and had spent his money on learning English and reading and writing. One of the books he read was about the history of unionism in the United States. This gave him the idea of organizing his people in a sort of labor camp. We told him that he could try this experiment. He asked that we pay him 10% of the payroll to pay for his expenses and the food. We agreed as it would be immensely helpful to have a reliable workforce. The results were better than we expected. Time passed, and we were quite satisfied until we started to hear some grumbling from the men. We then found out that he had not told the men that he got paid by the company for all his expenses. Instead, he required 10% of each man's wages to cover expenses. He also used various scare techniques to keep the men in the camp during the week–so much for conversion from Stone Age to our "advanced society!" It is interesting that there is always someone who wants to lead and outsmart the rest of the group for his own advancement. We had to discontinue this practice and slowly build up enough interest to form a good labor force. The company was successful in this effort. However, whether these people really were better off with this new arrangement is a valid question.

Suriname suffered from very poor government and an inadequate infrastructure for many years. Symptomatic of this was an incident that took place as our plane was circling over the Paramaribo airport, which was built by the US during World War II. The copilot told me there was some trouble with the landing gear. I said that the airport looked very modern and well equipped for any emergency. He said, "Don't go by looks. All the new fire equipment at the airport is incompatible as relatives of the prime ministers had been hired as purchasing agents. Each one had bought equipment without having any standard as to what to buy". Fortunately, the crew was able to straighten out the landing gear problem, and we arrived safely.

At some point during the construction of the Alcoa project, one of the American TV networks did some filming at the construction site. Emphasis was given to the environmental impact. They claimed that hundreds of animals would lose their lives once the sluices in the dam were closed so that a lake would be formed to power the turbines. The documentary became an instant hit in the US, and funds were raised to rescue the animals. The company was attacked for its callous behavior. I was in Suriname when the water began to rise to form the lake. Lots of well meaning people were there going around in boats to pick up animals and bring them to the shore of the lake. The shore was totally covered by the jungle, so they couldn't see what went on behind the trees. What happened was that, as soon as they unloaded the animals, the natives were waiting for them and killed a lot of them both for food and for the joy of hunting. What was seen on American TV was the rescue effort, and not what went on behind the trees. Sometimes, it is possible to try to do the right thing but, in the process, not take into account the local culture.

I gained a lot of practical experience, especially in trying to solve problems that dealt with people of different cultures and trying to deal with the types of issues that cannot be found in a textbook on finance or auditing or the principles of management. I was very impressed with the construction experts that Alcoa sent out to build this project in the middle of a jungle. They were ingenious and had that attitude of "we can do it, and we will!" We had some laughs, too. For example, in the jungle motel where we stayed, one of the employees was a young man who was an untrained housekeeper, but very friendly and willing to learn. One day a colleague asked him if he knew how to clean boots. He said that he did. That evening, when we returned from work, we found that he had put the boots in a bucket of water and cleaned them with soap. He had never heard of shoe polish. Another time, we were passing the big warehouse where the company stored most of its material and equipment. It was late at night and, all the lights were blazing. Electricity was very expensive before the dam was built. We were surprised. We knew there was only one night watchman on duty. When we went in, we asked him why all the lights were on. He answered that he was afraid of the dark. So much for our security system!

I had a varied and interesting time working almost full time on the Alcoa account. I reported to a manager at Lybrand who was excellent to work for. The sheer size of the company sometimes made small problems big and simple issues complicated. However, we had an excellent working relationship, and they respected our people and our work.

A number of years after my start with Alcoa, I was asked to audit a brand new plant that was automated both in the production line and in its administration. I had gone to school to learn the basics of computers and also had learned something about the control aspects of the computerized operations. The heart of the computer process was the software. The computer itself had, even in the early days, so many built-in checks and balances that the main weakness was the adequacy of the software and the skill of the operators. The new plant that I was to audit was so automated that it was difficult to understand the logic and safety features of the programs used. Even the manpower in that plant had been reduced to a negligible number. I actually had to go back to a manual calculation of: "with x units of raw material and y units of machine capacity, a production of z cans should be produced" and use these quantities to compare with the computer printouts. Fortunately, it all checked out pretty well, so we didn't have to dig too deep in a step by step approach to check out the programs. Ironically, the main problem the company had was the local union. Under the automated system, the workmen had to use IBM cards at each station and fill in the time they had worked and some detail about their work. Since that was never required of them before, the union took the position that the workmen now were also administrators and, therefore, should get a higher hourly rate. Overall, I enjoyed working and learning about the computer, and later lectured for the CPA society about auditing computer systems. I myself never acquired a computer until I retired, at which time I finally came to grips with the "user friendly" programs of the PC. With all the advances, I still found that term a misnomer.

By now, I had become well acquainted with the top management of Alcoa. I accompanied one executive to a visit at the huge Massena plant. He was an impatient man and was especially impatient with the small airline that served the area. On the return trip, we had to change planes in Syracuse, and he insisted that the pilot call ahead to make sure that the connecting plane in Syracuse would wait for us. This request was refused as, under government rules, planes were allowed only a minimum delay time, at least according to our flight attendant. My companion was fuming, but to no avail. Our plane was, as usual, late. However, when we checked in at Syracuse, we were told that the connecting plane was at the gate and that there was enough time for us to board in a leisurely fashion. My companion immediately left for the restroom, which was not in the immediate vicinity. Shortly after he left, the desk clerk called me and said that he had misinformed us. The plane was leaving immediately. I decided to run for the plane. As I climbed the staircase, which was part of the plane and not a detached ramp, I had the brilliant idea of stopping halfway up and waiting for my friend. The flight attendant got more and more angry because I was holding up the plane until my companion arrived. A few minutes later, I caught sight of him, but he was running to the wrong plane. I couldn't leave the stairs as the flight crew surely would immediately pull them up and leave. I screamed to get my companion's attention, and he finally responded. I saved the day for him. Later he explained to the flight attendant how much he appreciated them waiting for him. He reminded her that Alcoa was really the main customer of the airline and everything returned to a more peaceful state.

Another episode involving the top management at Alcoa involved their interest in expanding into Europe. I had been telling them that many Americans were still considered provincial by Europeans. I knew from experience that there was some kind of fear in the top corporate echelons in those days about expanding abroad. One day, when I was talking to the controller of Alcoa, he asked me if I would be a European tour guide for a group of senior officials. I was delighted! One of the stops I arranged was in Brussels. It so happened that my mother still lived there, and I thought that she could tour us around that city which is beautiful and interesting. I wrote to my mother, and she was very pleased to do that. She told me that my stepfather would take a day off and drive us around. That was a serious problem for me. The way the man drove was similar to the cartoon character Mr. Magoo. He managed frequently to go the wrong way on a one way street and, in general, drove like he owned the road. People in his car would be more worried about surviving than seeing the scenery. I wrote to my mother about my concern. As always, she came up with a diplomatic solution. She told him that it would be too strenuous for him to drive and explain the surroundings at the same time. She also told him that the three visiting Americans were typically big in size, and we would not all fit comfortably in the car. He agreed and rented a limousine and driver. The folks from Alcoa had a marvelous time and talked about this trip for a long time.

My private life in Pittsburgh was difficult. At Nancy's new home at Clelian Heights, one of the speech therapists there took an interest in her and worked with her for a year. Tests showed a slight injury in the left part of her brain which was the cause of her impaired speech and emotional problems. This changed Nancy's treatment regimen as the emphasis now changed to working with her on her speech. Her first intelligible words came around age eleven. We were thankful that this doctor had shown interest in Nancy far beyond the call of duty. At this time, we also had a second daughter Joyce. She was doing well, but we all were impacted by the stress created by our concern for Nancy. This was becoming a serious problem for my wife. She had many stressful moments and started to behave irrationally. She received psychiatric treatment and medication to make her more functional, but our marriage deteriorated seriously.

A son, John, also was born while we lived in Pittsburgh. When he was a one year old, he developed a rash on his head. Our pediatrician was away, and his substitute examined him. She told us not to worry, but a couple of days later, the rash started to spread rather rapidly. The doctor visited again, and now she was worried because she had no idea what was causing the rash. After a few more days, we had to take him to the hospital because the top layers of his skin started to peel off at an alarming rate. The hospital put him in complete isolation and turned his body every fifteen or twenty minutes to minimize the irritation of the contact between the linens and his skin. Our regular pediatrician had returned, and he admitted that he and his colleagues had never seen anything like this problem. The doctor pumped John full of antibiotics to the extent that it was a high risk whether a baby could absorb that kind of dosage. The case rapidly became rather well known and many doctors came to observe. After one week at the hospital, John had lost his top layer of skin from top to bottom. My brother, using his contacts as a doctor, called all over Europe to find somebody who had seen a case like that. He finally talked to a doctor in Ireland who claimed that there were several known cases with similar symptoms. All had died from the skin infection. My mother had insisted that, if anything serious was happening with any of us, that she should be informed. When the doctor told me that the disease had reached the critical stage and that our son could die within the next few days, I decided to call my mother. I will never forget that call from a pay phone in the hospital. Fortunately, my mother did not panic and was able to give me some comfort. The next day, the miracle happened. All of a sudden, there were signs that the skin was growing back and, a week later, most of the skin was back and there were no scars. Our pediatrician had been phenomenal. He had cancelled a big 25th wedding anniversary as he wanted to stay day and night with John. He told me that there is nothing worse for a doctor than not being able to identify the sickness, and therefore being helpless in prescribing the proper treatment. The case was written up in a medical journal, and fortunately my son had no lasting damage from this experience. Especially as you get older, you start to appreciate more the blessing of good health. We take it so for granted.

We made some nice friends in Pittsburgh. My boss was a very good friend. He came from a large family and told me that, after a number of years of marriage, they had hoped to have some children, but so far they hadn't had any luck. One day, his wife's brother and wife died, apparently in an accident. My boss adopted the only daughter and, since then, they had a baby each year, resulting in ten boys and one girl in all. It was an experience to eat at their home. They usually ate in installments. As a good accountant, he had set up a system by organizing a co-op that bought the food and other family needs. By having this co-op, they could purchase commodities at wholesale prices.

I also received a lot of support from the Presbyterian Church which was located right down the street. It was a very warm and outgoing congregation. The assistant minister was a retired Navy chaplain. He was accident prone, especially during the worship service. When he read from the Bible, he sometimes turned two pages without noticing it, thereby throwing us all into confusion. He never took it seriously when someone pointed out his errors. His sermons were not always inspiring. However, he told the congregation that he didn't mind if they fell asleep as long as they didn't snore.

One day, I came home from work and found our car dangling from a wall next to our driveway. The driveway had a steep decline from the road to the garage under the house and, somehow, Dorothy had made a short turn backing into the driveway and had, instead, missed the driveway and landed on the wall. I haven't mentioned some of the experiences I've had with cars. Before we moved to Pittsburgh, we lived in a ranch house in Natick, MA. We had a good-sized garage that had a screen which, in the summer, was used instead of the garage doors. I had read that you could spray the screen with paint so that you could sit in privacy in the garage, but people could not look in from the outside. I bought the spray paint and applying it was an easy job. When I finished, I turned around and noticed that my brother's black Pontiac was now gray. My brother and his wife were in Europe, and I was taking care of their two cars. He returned that evening, and I called him the next day and apologized for what had happened. I asked him to come and get the two cars. He couldn't do it that day, but asked if he could pick them up with his wife the following day. Then, the next day he called and asked if we could drive the cars back. His second car was a Hillman station wagon. It wouldn't start. I asked Dorothy to get in our car and gently push the Hillman until we reached about twenty miles per hour. She had never done this and thought that she should get her car up to twenty miles per hour first. You can image the rest of the story.

COOPERS AND LYBRAND–NEW YORK

After some five years in Pittsburgh, I was transferred to the main office in New York. There I joined a couple of thousand CPAs in the Lybrand office, which was in downtown Manhattan. It was a challenge to find a suitable place to live. I liked Long Island, but the driving was almost impossible. They called the expressway the longest parking lot in the world. It is also extremely expensive to live there. I got the home addresses of my colleagues and noted where most of them lived. I found New Jersey to be the preferred place. We bought a house in New Providence, also known as Murray Hill, which was famous as the home of Bell Labs. It was only twenty-five miles from Manhattan, so I figured commuting by car would be manageable. Was I wrong!! As a result, I ended up walking one block to the railroad station and then took the Erie Lackawanna train to Hoboken. The cars were so old that speeds over twenty miles an hour made the rail cars shake. Then I took the ferry across the Hudson and, after that, walked the rest of the way to the office. It took about one and a half hours to make the trip; to travel twenty-five miles!

The New York office was a brand new experience for me. It was so big that you could know only a small portion of your fellow employees. Also, because of the size, everything was much more bureaucratic. However, at the same time, you had the feeling that you were at the center of things. My new responsibilities were to be an assistant to the senior partner in charge of international accounts and to be an auditor for some of the domestic clients. My international work was extremely interesting. I had to design a format which would give our clients economic highlights for each country where we had a practice and also highlight the characteristics of the local culture, information about climate and living conditions. This information was regularly updated for our clients. I had been promoted in Pittsburgh from a senior position to supervisor, which meant that I got more involved in the assessment part of the audits rather than the routine details. I had oversight for some very large accounts, as well as some smaller ones.

My international experience with Alcoa, my multiple languages and my European background were very valuable with Lybrand's multi-national clients. I was a supervisor on the Chase Manhattan bank audit in charge of reviewing their entire foreign loan portfolio. This was a long way from being a starting auditor where you spend weeks in bank vaults counting securities. The files that I had to read for foreign loans could have been manuscripts for movies. They described the people, companies and special deals that had to be made to consummate a loan.

Another assignment involved the Reynolds Tobacco Company. They had just built a new building on Park Avenue. Rumor had it that they spent more on the interior offices, including expensive art, than on the rest of the whole building. I never found out if that was correct. I do know from having audited so many companies that executives have a great need to be physically recognized through the size, location and furnishing of their offices. I know of one company that bought a hotel in Switzerland for the headquarters of their European operation. The moving-in date was delayed for a year because not all of the executive offices had a private bathroom, and that was an important status symbol.

One day, I was called in by one of the partners who asked if I could go to Europe on short notice. One of the major clients of Lybrand, who was involved in construction world-wide, wanted to acquire a Dutch company and time was of the essence. They had already arranged my flight with KLM. Since this company had made such a priority about getting me there as quickly as possible, an executive from the KLM public relations department called me to see if there was anything they could do to make my trip more enjoyable. They must have thought that I was a VIP. I enjoyed the treatment while it lasted, which wasn't long. I was supposed to fly on Saturday morning. However, at 6:00 a.m., I received a telephone call to report that the deal had been postponed. However, I did make the trip later. The Dutch company was a solid company, but not wise to American know-how. I noticed that they closed the company for two weeks to do inventory. I analyzed the inventory, and found the usual–that about 20% of the inventory represented 80% of the dollar value. I explained that in the US, they would concentrate on the expensive items and do less testing on the low value items. Up until then, they had counted every screw and nail. I became an overnight hero. Over the years, I observed some interesting differences in public accounting between different countries. In the US, audit efficiency is emphasized, thereby keeping the cost down. In addition, becoming a CPA was more possible financially because, during your apprenticeship, you get a salary from the firm. In England, you didn't get paid, and therefore only the wealthy could afford to become a Chartered Accountant. Consequently, the Chartered Accountant in England had a very high standing and was used as business adviser while lawyers were much lower in the esteem of the business world. In the Netherlands, to become a CPA, you had to study for four years at a specialized university. It was considered one of the most difficult courses of study. When you graduated, many would go on to get a law degree and a degree in economics. People who followed this path were considered so far above the average that nobody argued with them. However, although the Dutch accountant was probably the best academically trained accountant in the world, they lacked the practical experience that their American counterpart had attained. The German accountancy experience was quite different again. Everything was regulated by law. Their work was done with such detail that I could not believe the volumes of audit work papers they generated, even with a small client.

An illustration of the English accountant in action comes from an audit I did with a staff supplied from London. The audit was in Switzerland. The team was excellent, and one staff member in particular stood out. On completion, I complimented him on a job well done. I told him that he would have a great future. He thanked me for the compliment. Upon my return to New York, I told my boss about this young man and said that I would write a letter to the London office about him. He laughed and said, "You know who that young man is? He is the son of the Chairman of the Board of ICI, one of the largest chemical companies in the world." I wrote the letter anyway. Everybody likes a compliment.

Meanwhile, I was promoted to audit manager and had a chance to see more of the overall management of the firm. I noted that, although Lybrand was by far the largest company in the international firm, the English partner Cooper Brothers seemed to have the dominant role in its management. I also observed that the international firm had not yet standardized the training of its members in each country. The lack of such standardized training led to unfortunate misunder-standings between our American clients and their subsidiary operations overseas. Most American clients thought that any of the big eight accounting firms could do the job. Since most of them had similar loose arrangements overseas, Lybrand could jump the gun by investing money in training all the affiliated foreign accounting firms in a standard audit procedure. This would also be a unique chance for me to move up the ladder in a way that I would enjoy. A senior partner told me that he agreed with my ideas, but that it was not the right time to implement them, especially since our company still had to come to terms with the English firm. It was a disappointment for me because I thought the timing was just right. Later on, the senior partner implemented the ideas and became the managing partner of the firm.

Family and Community Life–New York

At home things were not easy. My wife Dorothy's problems continued unabated. She was treated by a psychiatrist, but the only way he could help her was by providing medication that made her somewhat functional. She had been diagnosed as suffering from schizophrenia, among other things, leading to irrational behavior. She would often need instant gratification. If we went on a trip in the car, all of a sudden she wanted to stop for coffee. If there was no place to get coffee, she would quickly get very angry and uncontrollable. Several times, I had to restrain her in the car at the risk of losing control over the steering wheel. Her buying of food was haphazard, and we were constantly oversupplied in certain items and short of others. She became worried that a certain hairspray that she used would be discontinued at some point. I found more than sixty cans of hairspray in the closets.

Meanwhile, my daughter Nancy had been transferred to a state institution in Towata, NJ. They had a special education school and had many activities for the residents. They educated Nancy to her maximum level, which was the equivalent of a six year old. The problems of the brain and emotional problems are so complicated that, although medicine has made progress, doctors and health care workers are still very limited in what they can do. Nancy learned some skills doing crafts and knitting. She also helped in the nursery as an aide as she loved babies. We had a parent group that supported the institution. One couple in particular was outstanding. The wife set up a Girl Scout troop and took the girls on field trips and taught them many useful things. The husband was the president of the parents' group. Later, I became involved and took on this position. We raised money, organized parties and helped politically to gain support for the school. In order to provide spiritual support, we helped form an ecumenical ministry with a rabbi, a priest and a minister. They selected a hymnal for use at the school, developed a residents' choir and officiated at a Sunday morning service. Dorothy had a difficult time facing Nancy and mostly solved the problem by ignoring her existence. I tried to compensate by going to the institution most Sundays to spend time with Nancy.

However, there was no question that Nancy and the other handicapped kids needed all the help we could muster. I remember the extensive discussions we had when the federal government decided that these state institutions were much too big and isolated from the mainstream of the population. The government was proposing the initiation of a program to move these residents out into the community by providing smaller group homes or through private placement. If the states could make this happen, they could receive substantial grants from the federal government. The state saw this as a practical way to reduce their cost of providing for the mentally handicapped so they jumped on the band wagon. The parents' association felt that based on past performance, the government might start this with the best of intentions, but then might withdraw its support in the future and let the state carry the burden. Also, even if smaller group homes and privatization may be desirable, the cost per resident would be much higher. The mentally handicapped had very little representation in the political world, and we parents could only do so much. Unfortunately, the scenario went exactly as predicted, and many of the handicapped became homeless. It is a national disgrace what we have done to these helpless people.

I had a very busy life between my job and my activities on the school board and in the church. Of course, I tried to spend time with my children. Each Sunday, I drove an hour to get to Totowa, where Nancy resided. Since my marriage was so difficult, my participation in the outside activities may have been a way to avoid being with my wife. Unfortunately, it reached a point with Dorothy that my brother, who is a psychiatrist, advised that we should separate. He forecasted that her situation would continue to deteriorate and said that there was no known treatment to cure her. At the time, I felt that I had to stay with her as it would be devastating to my children to have a divorce. On reflection, I don't know whether my motivation was so noble. A possibility exists that my pride stood in the way. Divorce was like admitting failure. I continued to cover up our problems. Inviting people to our house was always a strain as Dorothy would be so uptight about guests that she would have extreme outbursts before the guests arrived or after the guests had left. She usually accused me of flirting with the ladies or saying things that made her look bad. It was interesting to note that, while guests were present, she could not engage in a personal conversation. The minute a conversation would go in her direction, she would drastically change the subject, many times surprising our friends. She also had an extreme concern about her appearance. She had excellent taste in clothes and was always dressed beautifully. Her hair was so perfect that she could not allow herself to relax. If it was windy, she wouldn't go out. On vacations, she wouldn't go swimming because afterwards her hair might not look right. I was only allowed to take a shower at certain times as the dampness might affect her hair. My feelings toward her became a combination of pity and frustration. During her temper tantrums, she would throw things at me, including knives and, one time, hot water. I became more experienced in restraining her physically, but sometimes I let my temper get control of me and overreacted. That led one time to her calling the police. Her skin was extremely sensitive and any firm grip by me would show dark spots on her skin. Fortunately, the policeman who came was able to calm her down and did not pursue any action against me. The horror of this was that my children were exposed to some of this, although most of the unfortunate happenings took place after they were in bed. Many times my wife was able and willing to defer her anger until that time. When I said that we should talk later about a problem, she often went along with the suggestion.

My second daughter, Joyce, had reached high school age and was very popular. As a parent, I was probably too strict. Many a boyfriend was shown to the door. Joyce had found a good job during her senior year with Sears and actually was doing so well that she had the possibility of a good career. She also started to date quite seriously.

She didn't want to go on to college. I had learned, to some degree, that I could not force her to change her mind. However, whenever the chance presented itself, I would discuss with her the merits of a college education. Sometime later, she announced that she was interested in going to Mount Ida College, which at that time was a two year liberal arts college in Boston. She did just that and met her future husband there as well.

My youngest daughter, Lani, caused us a laugh. When she was three years old, she played with a neighbor's son who was about the same age. One time we found them hidden, playing in a closet. We have teased her ever since that she started early with her boyfriends.

After having lived in various houses, my skills in carpentry or fixing things had really not improved. I seem to have a built-in impatience and a desire to find short cuts. One day, I went to a lumber store where they sold dog houses. I love dogs, and I thought that our dog should have its own dog house. When I talked to the salesman, he said that I didn't need to pay for a finished dog house. Even a child could build one easily. I took that as an immediate challenge. He drew a diagram and figured out the various items I would need. Full of optimism, I started the construction in our garage. Soon, I ran into some problems as I didn't remember his instructions perfectly. I went back to the lumber store and bought some more lumber. After using more and more of my own ideas on how to build it, I ended up with a fortress that could house two dogs. It even had carpeting and a front porch. When I tried to move it, I found that I needed to ask my neighbor for some help. We moved it as far as the fence to my backyard. I then realized that the dog house was too big to get through the gate. So, we got some more neighbors to help lift it over the fence. Despite my difficulties, it was so well constructed that, when we lifted it over the fence and by accident dropped it, it was not damaged. I then tried to entice the dog to enter the palace. I had even put some meat inside. The dog refused, and never used it!

One summer, Dorothy and I went to the Hollywood Hotel in New Jersey for a short vacation. The hotel was filled with a laundry industry convention. The participants were really whooping it up. We were invited to attend the grand ball. We accepted and, after a sumptuous dinner, they had a dancing contest where volunteers from the banquet would dance with someone from the professional dance troop that had been part of the entertainment during dinner. I volunteered to do a Dutch jitterbug. When I climbed on stage, I found that my partner, who from a distance looked dainty, was muscled like a football player. I had the courage to take on the challenge. My partner said she would just follow my lead. I was improvising, and she was a good trooper. I guess that I made an idiot of myself, but we won the first prize. When I returned to my table, a woman approached me and introduced herself as a talent scout for "Name That Tune". She told me that she had never seen anything like my dance. They always looked for characters to be on their television show. She invited me to come, and I accepted. I passed the interview, and the date was set for my appearance. My wife had bought a new outfit for the occasion, including a hat that cost more than the dress. When I went onstage, I was fairly nervous. The idea was that the orchestra would play a tune and, as soon as you recognized it, you would run to a big bell and ring it. If you could name the various tunes, you could win as much as $25,000. I heard the first song and ran to the bell. I had heard or played that song a thousand times on the piano. It was "My Blue Heaven". However, after I rang the bell, my mind went blank, and I said it was "Molly and Me". The host said, "I'm awfully sorry, that is not the correct answer". My opponent had the correct answer and won the first round while I was eliminated. That was the end of my television career.

That particular vacation was a memorable one. Near the hotel was a famous horse racing track. Dorothy and I had never been to a horse race. Upon entering, we were approached by a man with a big cigar. He could tell new customers from a mile away. He explained that he sold the inside story and, since he was very modest in his fee, I made a bet on the proposed horse. He then guided us to some seats where he and his wife were sitting. His cigar smoke blew right into our faces, which made Dorothy very uncomfortable. Then, his wife started to argue with him saying that his horse was never going to win and that he always lost money. However, the horse recommended by the man came in first, and his wife's horse came in third. I then found out that supposedly I hadn't selected the right option as there was a difference between "to win" and "to place". We had endured enough cigar smoke and lost money. We thought that we should beat the crowds and go back to the huge parking lot and leave before all the races were over. It started to pour so that, by the time we found our car, we were soaked. Once we had located our car, we found that it wouldn't start. It had a dead battery. I walked back to the entrance. The attendant said that, after everybody had left, a tow car would come around to help the stranded. All told, it was a disappointing experience and one never to be repeated.

We joined a Presbyterian church in the neighboring town of Summit. We especially enjoyed the music program, and I joined the choir. The church had one of the top organists in the area who also led the choir. His wife was a well-known singer and helped to direct the choir and the children's choirs. The director was very inspiring and encouraged us to compose our own anthems and choral responses. I wrote a few and found it exciting to hear my own music sung in the church. Unfortunately, the music director became so popular that the senior minister felt that he was upstaging him in the Sunday service. This became a most unpleasant fight, and the congregation got more and more involved. Finally, the board insisted that at least the wife of the director should step back from her role in the church music program. The organist refused and was ultimately let go. I was crushed to see the petty jealousies at work in a Christian environment. I think that the challenge for a member of a church is to help resolve the issue. I had tried to do that in this church, but ran into a stone wall with the minister. He couldn't recognize that a good music program would enhance the religious experience, and it was not a contest to see who is the most popular. I have always found it disappointing that the strength of a congregation often falls because of a lack of tolerance and narrow opinions.

We left the Summit church and joined a much smaller Presbyterian church in New Providence. They had just installed a new minister. He had been brought up in the Jewish faith, but as an adult, had converted to Christianity. He was a very energetic and bright person and saw his ministry as a missionary effort as he endeavored to build up the congregation. He was very supportive of a good music program and was very forthright in his opinions. His sermons were of such quality that, after a while, members started to return. The church didn't have much money for a music program, but a miracle happened. A candidate came forward to inquire about the opening. He had been the director of the Newark Boys Choir which had an outstanding reputation. He liked our minister and was encouraged by the talent in our small choir. When he became the music director, he treated us as professionals. We had to show up on time for rehearsals, and talking among choir members was not allowed during rehearsals. His knowledge and ability was enormous. He could play the organ and direct the choir with skill and musicality. It was a joy to work with him. Soon, more people started to join the choir, and we were able to produce programs of such quality that there was standing room only at the services.

Church was very important to me. With all the tensions and anxieties at home, it gave me some strength to endure. We had small groups within the membership of the church that met regularly. These groups built up the type of relationships where we didn't have to put up a front and could talk about our real personal problems. One couple in my group was an inspiration. The husband had climbed the corporate ladder in a large chemical company and had narrowed his vision so that the only thing that mattered to him was to become the president of the company. He had reasoned that, by amply providing his family with all the things they needed, he had done his job to make it a happy family. When he achieved the position of senior vice president, his wife insisted that he take a week off to have some personal time with her. He had loved her in his own way all his married life and asked why she wanted to do this. She replied that she felt their marriage was totally unsatisfactory as he only provided "things" and nothing else. She told him that, unless he could change and spend more time with the family, she would leave him. He was in shock. They spent the week talking, and he realized without a doubt that his family was more important than his pride and his work. He quit his job and decided to start a consulting service three days a week. The rest of his time would be devoted to his wife and children and to active participation in the church. As he was well known in the industry, he was able to start his consultancy with the help of former business connections. Because of his expertise, he could charge market rates. In no time, his consultancy prospered. In the three days a week that he worked, he made more money than previously. God works in mysterious ways. He and his wife were like honeymooners and shared their faith.

As Joyce was now a senior in high school, I was getting more and more concerned about her lack of knowledge or interest in world events and her ignorance in so many basic subjects. I asked her to invite twelve of her classmates to our house for a party, at which time I would give them a short test to see whether they had the same deficiencies. I asked them some basic questions. For example, I asked the name of the secretary of state–Henry Kissinger at the time. Only a few could answer that question correctly. That showed how little they read the front page of a newspaper. I asked them which country they associated with the name Napoleon Bonaparte. Only two attendees knew. The same dismal results were shown in spelling, knowledge of word meanings and basic arithmetic. It was astounding to me.

I decided to run for the school board. I had never before run for any elected office. Some experienced friends helped, and I appreciated their help. I soon found out that, in politics, relationships and name recognition seem to be as important as substance. I made a lot of visits to neighbors who had invited their friends to hear about what I was planning to do to address problems in the schools. Many questions were raised. I think we were all uninformed about what we could do to improve the educational system. However, it appears that one needs that kind of enthusiasm and ignorance about the realities of the educational process to be able to make appealing statements that will lead to being elected. In my case, I wrote articles, and then my two closest advisers would turn them completely around. They claimed I would not get elected otherwise. What they did was to add slogans and campaign gimmicks to an otherwise reasoned article. Even after all the campaigning, it is amazing how few people in town went through the trouble of voting. However, I did win the election.

After joining the board, I found out that the superintendent was quite persuasive in explaining to us that we knew very little about education. He urged us to rely on his expertise to make the right judgments. We, of course, questioned that premise, but found that, in most cases, he did know better because of his many years of experience. I felt that the board should stay out of the day to day battles and spend time on overall objectives. Since there were no standards or qualifications to become a board member, we had a great variety of people on the board. One member was a housewife. She was obviously well educated, but had some extreme ideas. She maintained that it was necessary that she read every new textbook that the school wanted to purchase. I asked her if she was knowledgeable in all the subjects, and she said she was not. However, she still felt that, even if she didn't understand the text, she felt an obligation to read the entire book. This caused unnecessary delays, but she would not budge.

The public board meetings were even more frustrating. The attendees were often complaining mothers. In some cases, if they didn't get anywhere with their complaints, the father would show up or sometimes even a lawyer. I found that the minute you became a public official, people became suspicious of your motives. Some parents had a one-sided emotional view and were unwilling to listen to reason. Others liked to come to make public speeches. We had to learn to keep calm and listen respectfully to whatever a parent would say. This was very difficult for me because I knew in many instances how wrong they were. This was especially difficult when the father was brought in. Unfortunately, in many families, the mother had the sole responsibility for the education of the children. The father came in totally unprepared other than what his wife had told him. In most cases, he would not have talked directly with the teacher or other officials. He would make grandiose statements and often would try to make an impression by saying that, if what was bothering them in the school system had happened in his business, everyone would be fired. They always insinuated that we, as members of the school board, all had some sort of sinister motives.

In reality, we did not get paid and worked an unbelievable amount of time, particularly during negotiations with the teachers union. Another challenge was that the state of New Jersey had ruled that raising money for the schools through real estate taxes was inequitable and unconstitu-tional. It took the legislature some years to come up with a new system. Meanwhile, all the school boards in the state were floundering as they had no idea how much money would be available for the next year. I believe that the state, through the Secretary of Education, did an excellent job in coming up with a solution that gave towns more equitable funding and also made steps to monitor the educational results in each town. The Board of Education system really needed overhauling, and more effective standards needed to be adopted in order to get more qualified people elected. I grew up in Holland where the state was totally responsible for education. That system had problems too. However, some qualified monitoring of local boards by a carefully selected public board could be useful.

A number of summers we went to Lake Kasagawiggemar in Canada, north of Toronto. We would stay there for a week and enjoy the simple, but beautiful life. We stayed in a small lodge run by a unique couple from Great Britain. The husband was the entertainer. A great athlete, he gave water-skiing exhibitions by skiing without skis on one foot and, at the end of the show, he would get close enough to the beach that he could walk ashore. There was entertainment each night. In the winter, the owner took unbelievable pictures of the animals and the snow and the plants. On the first day, he took us in his motorboat to a small inlet of the large lake. He then turned the engine off and told us to be completely quiet and listen to nature. He explained that, because we lived in the city, our ears would not easily pick up the sounds of nature. It took several minutes before I started to hear various birds and the noise of some beavers that were nearby. Another beautiful aspect of the place was that it brought people together, and the art of conversation was rediscovered. I have a lot of wonderful memories from this place and the people we met there.

HUNTINGTON HARTFORD

One of Lybrand's clients was Huntington Hartford. He used Lybrand as a consultant and randomly called various partners for advice. Many times the questions didn't warrant the use of a partner's time. However, by doing this, he ended up running up a substantial bill. The partners were a little embarrassed about it and asked me to become the anchor man in dealing with him. I also had to do an annual audit of his holding company. When I did the audit, I could not believe the variety of financial interests the man had. Many were quite interesting, but poorly handled. As a result, he had to regularly make substantial write-offs. When I sat down with him to talk about my findings, I told him that, when a man earns ten thousand dollars and then spends twenty thousand dollars, he has a problem. I said, "In your case, when you earn ten million dollars and spend twenty million, you also have a problem".

He liked my frankness and, after studying more of my findings, he insisted that I should work for him. He offered me double my salary and the use of his homes in London, New Jersey and the Bahamas. The offices, at the time, were in the A&P building above Grand Central Station. I told him that I would think about it. I knew that it would be some time before I could be considered to become a partner. However, I also knew from previous experience that it could be risky to work for a single individual. I knew that the job would be a great challenge and that I would meet a lot of interesting and prominent people. My ever existing need for funds to cover family expenses was also a pertinent factor. I accepted.

The next five years in my career with him were exhausting, exciting and totally beyond my wildest imagination. I had told him that the only way I could be of use to him was for him to consider me as a brother. He should take any of my advice as coming from an independent person who was honest enough to consider the welfare of his boss as his foremost goal. I had talked to some of the people he had employed and the picture was clear. He would patiently listen to others, but then would completely follow his own intuition.

He was an intelligent man and had a good education. He graduated from Harvard. He was a good athlete; tennis was his forte. He took good care of his physical well being and hardly drank any liquor and didn't smoke. Winters were spent in Palm Beach. His two uncles, who had no children, took an interest in him as he was to be groomed to be the heir apparent to take over the A&P, but it did not work out.

When Huntington was 45, his mother died and, all of a sudden, he had to manage his own financial wealth of about one hundred million dollars. He had never managed any finances as his mother took care of everything for him right up until her death.

His business enterprise had a small staff of extremely devoted ladies, most of who had always worked for the family in one way or another. The woman in charge of the office had been his mother's secretary. The second in command was an extremely bright woman who had the task of turning away the many promoters who came to him to pry some money away. Another woman had previously been employed as a servant, and now was the Girl Friday of the office. Everybody worked long hours, and there was little or no frivolity. Huntington rarely came to the office. The lady in charge was very patient and uncomplaining and forthright. She certainly didn't approve of some of the things he got involved in. Hartford told me that he wanted to turn the business management totally over to me and basically gave me carte blanche over all his money, including the ability to sign checks of any amount. If I remember correctly, he came to my office about twice a year. The result was that I spent a lot of time at his home to get his attention.

One of my first assignments was to represent him at the annual stockholders meeting of the A&P. He agreed to attend, but I was to be his mouthpiece. He wanted me to give a speech at the annual meeting criticizing the A&P management. He told me to go and talk to one of his main investment bankers, Lehman Brothers. As he had a large account at Lehman Brothers, they paid attention. We crystallized main points to be used in my speech. My speech argued that changes should be made so that we have date stamps on the merchandise, indicating an expiration date and show a unit price. Also, since there was a large amount of traffic in the stores, some more profitable items should be added to the product lines since the markup on food was very low.

To give some background on the company, the uncles had built up the stores primarily in the twenties by inventing the idea of self service, thereby reducing costs. They were still deliberating who should be the heir when they died. They were not sure at the time and decided that their male secretary should take over. This would be a temporary solution until they could decide on the final choice, which presumably would be my boss. However, the uncles died unexpectedly and their male secretary became the new president. When I got into the picture, it became clear to me that the company was going downhill. Every organization has to face up to the needs and changing demands of the customer. Hartford, who every year had been the main criticizer of the management now had very legitimate reason to criticize the company.

When I appeared at the annual meeting, I was anxious. The press, including the Wall Street Journal and major trade papers, was there. Because of Hartford, they always wanted an interview with him and, in this case, with me as well. At the start of the proceedings, I had asked for the floor, but the chairman said that another person could speak first. The speaker was the president of the Women Stockholders of America. She was famous for her biting criticism of the male dominated business world. She went into a long harangue about the age of board members. She asked for each one to stand up and state his age. It was a comedy show. When it was my turn, board members were already a little uncomfortable. I was uncomfortable too, as I didn't know what to expect. They were very polite, but explained, in answer to my proposals, that it was not possible or practical to follow my suggestions. My only satisfaction was that, years later, supermarkets implemented these ideas.

Working for Hartford was a whole new environment for me. Since he was well known because of his wealth and life style, he attracted every promoter known to man. Some of these people were very bright and would have done well making a legitimate living. I found from experience that the better the story they presented, the more we had to be on guard for the real catch. Some people were pitiable. I had been there only a short time when a man came to present me with a proposal. He claimed to be a friend of Hartford's and was very persistent. I found out later that everybody claimed to be Hartford's friend because he was very accessible and very involved in public life. It was difficult to sort out who was legitimate. This person came dressed very oddly. He had purple socks and sort of orange slacks and a bright colored shirt. When he came in, he asked if he could close the door as he didn't want anybody to hear what he had to say. He then almost whispered and told me that he was a composer. He had worked for over twenty years on a musical that was so powerful that he needed to rent twenty pianos to give a proper rendition to potential producers. He claimed that his music was so good that a lot of his compositions had already been copied; thus, the secrecy. My main objective was to get him out of the door without getting him too upset. I had never dealt with people like him and was thinking of my Lybrand days where everything was very sedate and conservative. I devised an emergency solution that I have often used since then. I told him that what he had told me was very interesting, but that it would take some research and thought to evaluate his music and his proposal. He told me that he couldn't leave the music with me as he was afraid of plagiarism. I told him that I had rules that I had to go by and that it was absolutely necessary to get a copy of the music. He left quite upset, but at least there was no physical violence. I never heard from him again.

I slowly became familiar with the numerous investments that had been made which had a range that was hard to believe. When he inherited his money, he used a major law firm in New York to give him business, legal and financial advice. Since he was never sure whether or not he got the right advice, he had a habit of also getting other consultants to help him. Some were very prominent like the senior partners from Lehman Brothers or Lybrand. However, he also talked about his financial projects to people he might have met at a party. Therefore, he got such a wild range of advice that he had a difficult time making decisions. It was my primary job to analyze the facts and discuss with him the risks and merits of the various proposals that came his way. It was good that he had accepted the idea that I could talk to him like a trusted equal and not as an employee clerk.

After he received his inheritance, he spent the winter in Palm Beach. He usually was very bored as he didn't like the stuffiness of the residents at that expensive place. So, he and a cousin rented a yacht and sailed to Nassau. He was fascinated with the beauty of an undeveloped island called Hog Island. He inquired around and found that the island was owned by an elderly doctor. He looked him up and offered to buy the island. The doctor wanted six million dollars. On the back of an envelope, he wrote: "I owe you six million dollars for the purchase of Hog Island". He signed the envelope, and then called his lawyers to inform them what he had done. They were in shock. A senior partner moved heaven and earth to get the deal undone, but to no avail.

Hartford had a grand vision to develop this island into a premier resort. He contracted with a leading architect to come up with a master plan. The architect did draw up a plan but, as later proven, he had no business sense. His plans for island development showed no return on investment over a reasonable time span. The initial plan called for installing a drainage system, roads, power, a country club and a small hotel. The compound would appeal to the rich and would be basically set up as a tennis club. They went ahead with the plans and, after spending an additional twenty-eight million dollars, they had completed the master plan. However, there was no easy access to the island other than by boat. Hartford had tried everything to convince the Bahamian government to build a bridge, arguing that it would help the local economy by opening up this resort to the tourist trade. He had spent all this money and had no return on investment to show for it. The hotel was inaccessible, though beautiful. It was called the Ocean Club, but was too small to be economically productive.

When Hartford finally decided that he couldn't continue to develop the island alone, he made a deal with Resorts International. This company was originally known as the Mary Carter Paint Company and was owned by the Crosby family. The paint business was apparently not profitable, so Crosby had been looking to build a resort with gambling as the main attraction.

Jim Crosby was a very bright man with formidable negotiating skills. He could scream, flatter, twist and smile–changing from one state to another in an instant. Crosby struck a deal to take over what is now Paradise Island. Resorts International made big money through what was then the largest gambling casino in the world. When Hartford made his deal with Crosby, he didn't have much leverage because he had not earned any money with his investment in the island. Crosby was very shrewd and negotiated a deal with the Bahamian government whereby they would get a share of the casino earnings. In return, the government gave Crosby a license to build a hotel and a casino, but even more importantly, a permit to build a bridge from Nassau to Paradise Island. Crosby was allowed to collect a toll which, in time, brought in enough money to pay for the cost of the construction of the bridge.

As part of the island sale agreement, Hartford was made a board member of Resorts International. Since he didn't attend formal board meetings of Resorts International, I had to represent him. This was a most difficult task as his interests and Crosby's were miles apart. Hartford was very concerned about aesthetics, and Crosby's main concern was to make money. When the hotel was built on the island, Hartford felt that the building didn't fit in well with Bahamian architecture. They had built a typical tropical Holiday Inn type structure with a few luxury touches. Hartford thought that it looked cheap. He thought that the roof line was particularly offensive. He took me on a tour of Manhattan in his car to show me his idea of how the problem could be solved. He thought that having a certain kind of fence on the roof could soften the contour. He drove down the East River Drive and, when he saw a roof fence that he liked, he would stop the car right in the middle of the road. I was more concerned that we would get killed by blocking traffic on the major artery. Even when we were moving, it was scary as Hartford would look with half an eye on the road and, with the other half, look up at the roofs. His direction to me was to tell the board that he insisted that they build a fence on the roof. Hartford was very adamant and, with his vote, could block any other decision. Crosby decided that it was not worth his time to fight it, and the fence was built. It certainly made the hotel look more attractive.

Round two came when Hartford decided that, with the prices they charged at the hotel, they should serve real orange juice and not the frozen kind. I went through the same negotiation harangue. It seemed like it took forever to get the matter settled. We had lawyers and private summit meetings between Hartford and Crosby, which almost became fist fights. The matter was finally settled in Hartford's favor.

Meanwhile, I had found an extremely sharp investment banker to help me in dealing with all these problems. He was as tough as Crosby and certainly not intimidated by the man. After some years of hard negotiating, we finally made a deal with Crosby, which would be in the best interest of Hartford to accept. We then needed to convince Hartford, and the negotiations with him went on constantly. We even met in Acapulco where he was vacationing and entertaining Lyndon Johnson's brother as a guest. During the second day of these heavy meetings, which for some strange reason included President Lyndon Johnson's brother Sam, we had to stop because of the noise of a low flying plane which circled right above us. The plane was pulling a banner which read "Happy Birthday Sam Johnson". Apparently he was paid to keep circling for a long time. However, finally we could resume. Hartford could not make up his mind and kept procrastinating. Finally, in principle, he agreed to the final deal which, in our opinion, was a very favorable deal for him under the circumstances. Soon afterward, he met a new acquaintance who told him not to sign the deal. So, the deal was off. This was toward the end of my relationship with him, and soon thereafter, I left his employ.

Hartford told me an amusing story about a date with Zsa Zsa Gabor. He liked the glamour, but was not particularly interested in her. One day they had a dinner date, and they went to one of the society restaurants in Manhattan. Hartford had also invited four other people. Zsa Zsa was fuming as she didn't want them around because then she would not be the center of attraction. She got quite upset and the maître d' was called in to arbitrate. As a solution, a round table was attached to a square table. Zsa Zsa and Hartford would sit at the round table, and the rest of the party would be seated at the square table.

Publishing was another of Hartford's interests. Before I worked for him, he had published a very glossy magazine called Show Magazine. The magazine was staffed by well known professionals, and they apparently had carte blanche with regard to spending. It was a magazine for the performing arts and was very impressive. However, after losing a lot of money, he had to stop publishing it. After I started working for him, he told me that he was seriously thinking of starting the same type of magazine again. I did some research and counseled him against it, but he was determined to do it. I found that once he wanted something, he had to have it. I suggested that I should be heavily involved, particularly in controlling the money. He agreed to that arrangement. I suggested that we find a publisher with an established track record. After a search, we found that the current manager of Variety was interested in the job. We also found an editor with a solid background in that field. Hartford hired an interesting assistant editor who, years earlier, was the host for a famous radio show, "The Hit Parade". A lot of preparatory work, including a workable budget, went into this venture. Finally the day came to announce the official opening of the new Show Magazine. Hartford was going to give the best party of the New York season at the Inn of the Clock, a very fashionable restaurant on the east side of Manhattan. A key part of the planning involved inviting a famous personality as the centerpiece of the party. The party was going to be a black tie affair by invitation only. A couple of weeks before the party, the editor called me and said that he was resigning. He told me that Hartford had just called him to tell him that he had hired Tiny Tim to be the star. He said that he was not the right person. It was going to be a disaster to use him to reflect the image of the magazine. I agreed, but told him to hold off as I was going to talk to Hartford and see if I could change his mind. I spoke with Hartford and told him that hiring Tiny Tim gave too narrow an image about his magazine content. He should hire a few other types of entertainers to broaden the picture. I knew that he would go for that as he certainly thought that his magazine was the ultimate show business magazine. Hiring more stars would be costly. However, we went ahead with the plan, and the editor was delighted.

The choice of other attendees was my responsibility. Hartford expected a lot of freeloaders would try to get in as it was the talk of the town to be at this event. I had three women assisting me, and everything went well until I was told that the chairman of one of the major networks had arrived, but was not dressed in evening wear. I talked to the man, and he explained that he had just come from out of town and wanted to attend, but had no time to go home to change. I told him that I had strict orders, but that I would talk to Hartford. I did and, to my surprise, Hartford insisted that he had to go home and change his clothes. I said, "The whole idea of the party is to get these leaders interested, and this ultimatum will surely turn this man off". Hartford would not budge and, typically, would not tell him about his decision himself. He said that was my job. The man was outraged and left. Since a lot of people from the press were at the party, word got around quickly. The ironic part of the story was that, because of this incident, the episode and the party made headlines in the newspapers and elsewhere. It was not the type of publicity we wanted. However, the name of the magazine was prominently displayed in the media.

Another typical Hartford incident occurred when we went to Hollywood to have Hartford meet the press to officially announce the opening of the new magazine. We stayed at a famous landmark hotel, and Hartford was in a separate cottage. Hartford had lived in Hollywood and had made a significant impact on the area by building the only legitimate theater in Hollywood, The Hartford Theater. Hartford had also sponsored a camp which invited talented young writers to stay and perfect their skills. When the morning arrived for the press meeting, the first thing that went wrong was that the only time that it could be held was at eight in the morning. Hartford had developed his own lifestyle, which was to start the day at about eleven. He asked me and others to call him early to make sure he was ready. He also left a message with the hotel that he did not want to be disturbed. In the morning, I knocked on his door, and he answered. He explained that he had had a bad night as the room service was totally horrible. He had called at midnight for a glass of warm milk. After some wait, they brought him cold milk. He sent it back and waited again. They told him that there was no facility at night to heat the milk. Hartford then called the night manager and insisted that he get service. He finally got his warm milk, but most of the night had passed. He didn't want to have the press corps wait too long, so he showed up for the battery of cameras in his pajamas, robe and slippers. Again, that made the headlines, but not in the way we had wanted to announce the magazine.

I learned after a while that there was really no way to make the magazine financially viable. One reason was that Hartford really saw himself as an experienced editor and writer. Therefore, he argued about each issue as to what should be included and how it should be presented. It was exasperating for the staff as they had to meet the deadlines and many times disagreed with Hartford's ideas. It also cost a lot of money to change layouts and articles. The other problem was that Hartford used the magazine to reward some of his girlfriends who wanted to be in show business and, therefore, wanted to have their picture in the magazine. Hartford was a very literate man. As a matter of fact, he has been quoted in Webster's dictionary for definitions of some words. Nevertheless, his very strong feelings about his magazine made life very difficult for his staff which resulted in a high turnover.

However, the real death knell came through an incident that was not caused by him or his staff. A substantial amount of money and effort is necessary to make a magazine known to the public. The more readers there are, the more advertising revenue that can be charged. A special mailing was organized timed to maximize results. This is a very sophisticated aspect of the advertising business as both the material and the timing have to be very carefully thought out. Everything went very smoothly until the day of the mailing. That day turned out to be the day that the post office went on strike. We had to close the publication once again, but this cost us a lot less than the first time. Later on, Hartford tried once again with a smaller version of the magazine, but it just did not work.

Hartford was a well-known figure in the theatre world. His first wife was a Broadway star, and he had financed many plays and movies. One of his success stories was his underwriting of Jane Eyre. During my stint with him, he called me one day all excited. He said, "Jim, I just read one of the most interesting scripts I have ever seen, and I want to underwrite it". I said, "Hunt, I don't know anything about show business. What do you want me to do?" He said, "Go to my lawyer, who is the leading lawyer in the field with respect to the negotiating of a Broadway show. After that, you deal with the producer". I spent an hour with the lawyer, and then went to see the producer. Hartford was in a hurry, as he wanted to make sure that somebody else didn't beat him to the prize. The producer was a very good and honorable man, and it didn't take him long to find out that I knew little or nothing about this business. However, I felt that I could trust the man, and I actually enjoyed working with him. In my business career, I found many times that my judgment of people was fairly accurate and that I could follow my instincts. The name of the play was, "Does a Tiger

Wear a Necktie?" It was written by a man who had spent a year in a mental hospital to observe what was going on between patients and staff. The cast was excellent, but not well known. Before opening night, a group of psychiatrists were invited to make their comments. They were full of praise for the author as he had painted a realistic picture of what went on in the world of mental illness. Unfortunately, the critic of The New York Times felt otherwise, and the play was panned. The power of that particular critic was unbelievable. Nevertheless, two of the actors, Dustin Hoffman and Al Paccino, received a Tony.

After becoming more familiar with Hartford's operation, it became clear that one of the major problems he had was that he could not trust many people. This was not surprising. When you are known to be rich, everybody flatters you while aiming, at the same time, to get something out of you. Another problem might have come from his guilt about his enormous wealth. He wanted to do something for others. He was a leader in the Save the Met campaign to conserve the old Metropolitan opera building. Later, when the A&P workers were on strike, Hartford joined them in the picket line.

Another time, he got into an extended fight with Major Lindsay of New York. Hartford wanted to build a restaurant in Central Park. He lost that fight with the city. However, he didn't give up on the idea of having a restaurant in Manhattan. During my time with him, he had scouts looking for an authentic river boat which could be anchored in the East River and converted to a restaurant. This had been tried previously. To obtain the necessary licenses from a myriad of city agencies was considered more difficult than winning World War II. His agent found a boat in Chicago. Since Hartford didn't fly, he had pictures made and approved the purchase based on the visual evidence. The boat had to be trucked to New York, a very expensive and slow operation. However, to everybody's surprise, the move was successful. The boat was to be moored at an excellent location near Fifty-Ninth Street. Finally the boat arrived, and Hartford went to inspect it. He didn't like it and, on the spot, the whole deal was scrapped.

Later on, he decided that he was going to start a restaurant nightclub for middle age customers with the best sound equipment and music and gourmet food. He found a place on Lexington Avenue in the midtown area. We negotiated with a well-known company to be the leading partner in this venture. The site was rebuilt into a swanky English pub. The sound equipment was personally selected by the president of a major sound equipment manufacturer who also personally supervised its installation. He told me that there was nothing like it in the world. The volume could be turned up to the maximum, and there would still not be a disagreeable sound. Hartford then hired a man to research the best possible music selections in the US and in Europe. He built an extensive music library. By investing such an extraordinary amount of money in this place, it became more and more clear that recovering his investment was going to be a serious problem. Hartford didn't look at it that way. When he did something, it had to be the best and not a cheap commercial operation. Finally the nightclub was opened. He had a spectacular party and everybody was highly complementary. It was again true to Hartford's destiny that it was a great success, but it failed commercially.

Hartford didn't have real friends. I sincerely tried to be a friend, but his compulsions were so overwhelming that he really wanted to have people merely agree with him. I had never experienced close-up what lots of money can do to a person. His money seemed to create a distrust of others. There must also be some feeling of guilt for having so much money without any effort on his part. By not having to work for a living, the joy of trying to make it on your own is taken away. The rich and famous always seem to be the center of attention. In reality, Hartford was a very private person in many ways. However, he liked women, and therefore, was mercilessly harassed by the press. It got so bad that once, when he was in Paris, he met a well-known actress in the street and had a brief chat with her. The next day it was reported that he had had an affair with the woman. He called me from Paris and wanted to have the New York paper apologize. We talked with the editor and threatened to sue. The paper retracted the article, but apologized in such a way that the apology was worse than the article. I believe that it is extremely difficult to be born rich with everything done for you and all material needs fulfilled but, lacking real tender loving care, be able to make something of your life. It seems to me that when you are rich, you need much more discipline and moral fortitude than the average citizen. People are jealous of rich people, but I am not so sure that a man like Hartford enjoyed life or had a feeling of real accomplishment even though, in his own way, he tried very hard.

Having everything served on a silver platter and being totally protected by his mother until he was 45 must have been a handicap that restricted his whole life. I believe that the craving for being popular with women was one of the outcomes. He paid dearly for that, as he was crucified in the press and actually was honest enough to tell any female who wanted to have a serious relationship with him that he was not the marrying type. Nevertheless, he succumbed to marriage four times and each one was a disaster. His three children suffered as a result. He had a beautiful daughter who was doing well in school, but was slowly going into a decline. Hartford would spend any kind of money on schools, buying them all they wanted, but didn't really give his children much attention. If they wanted to talk to him, they had to wait in the living room until he had some time. The wait could be hours, or they had to come back the next day. On the other hand, he wanted to know where they went at night and, if he didn't know, he would use a detective to spy on them.

Hartford was amazingly ingenious in finding dates and surrounding himself constantly with attractive women. He helped to develop one of the leading modeling agencies in the country which, in turn, gave him access to the models. His Show Magazine also had a prominent display of beautiful women, which he had interviewed or selected.

Meanwhile, his urge to do good things for society had taken on some interesting twists. Since he was so interested in tennis, he wanted to develop the sport in the public schools. However, he realized that the schools didn't have the space or the funds to really develop the sport. He developed a game called "Double Up". It used a table almost twice the size of a ping pong table, a "nerve ball" made of foam rubber or other soft material and a small tennis racket. It had a similar stroke to tennis, but it didn't need the space or incur the cost of building a court. He developed it in his usual thorough way and had an employee researching every major ball manufacturer in the world to come up with the right size and the right composition for the ball. The player should be able to hit it hard and the ball should have enough bounce to jump over the net and yet be safe to use in a confined space. He had some of the top tennis pros come to test and play, and I was fortunate to meet and play with them. When he finally was satisfied with the technical aspects, he had a number of "Double Up" games made and donated to schools in the Bahamas, where they became quite popular in the seventies. When it came to marketing in the US, it was unsuccessful, despite substantial effort and cost.

In another venture, Hartford met an engineer from South Africa who was looking to find a sponsor for his invention. He had developed a motorized surf board. The idea was that many people in the US living in the Midwest cannot afford to go to the east or west coast to enjoy surfing. By having a motorized surf board, they could surf on any lake. Hartford agreed to finance further development. At that time, I was still new on the job, but believed that the two men were legitimate and that the idea might have commercial value. I think that my inexperience in developing this type of venture didn't help me to give proper guidance. The developer was totally committed to making it a success. However, when it came to testing the first real prototype, we found that there were some serious flaws. The little engine was mounted under the board for safety reasons. This meant that it could not be air cooled. However, it needed to stay cool so that the board would stay cool enough for someone to stand on it. The other problem was that it should shut off automatically in case something went wrong. They continued to work at the design. It was decided to have a small factory build surf boards. We kept putting money into the venture while, at some point, I should have counseled Hartford to take our losses and get out. Instead, we stayed with it, and a successful model was finally developed. By this time, Hartford had lost interest in the deal, but reluctantly stayed with it. We were once again faced with the enormous cost of marketing a new product. This time, Hartford put his foot down, and we did not go ahead with the venture. We were able to sell the invention to a cosmetic company which was diversifying and was building a resort in the mid west complete with a manmade lake with artificial waves where the surfboard could be put to use.

Another ingenious Hartford idea was to bring great works of art to the United States so that people who could not afford to go abroad could enjoy them. He contracted with a well-known photographer to make life-size photos of a mural painted by the famous Mexican artist Diego Rivera, a painter who concentrated on society's social problems.

The photographer did a superb job and a replica life-size mural was built and shown in the Hartford Museum in New York where it was a great success. Later, during my time with Hartford, we made a very interesting arrangement with Capital Cities Broadcasting Company. This company was extremely profitable, and it had established a policy that part of its profit should be spent for the common good. We negotiated a deal with them for a very unusual undertaking. The Sistine Chapel had recently been featured in a major magazine. As was usual, the photos had been taken from the ground. Since the ceiling in the Sistine Chapel is very high, the dust accumulated over the centuries has distorted the colors. Nobody really knew what the real colors were as the Vatican didn't allow the use of scaffolding to get close to the ceiling. However, Hartford was able to get a special permit to have scaffolding put in the chapel for a short period at which time the photographer could take pictures. The results were astonishing. The colors seen from below and the real colors were strikingly different. The shapes of the hands and the figures also appeared different because of the distance. The photographs were magnified to the actual size of the painting and now, for the first time in centuries, the actual painting of Michael Angelo could be seen. The photographs were put on exhibition and toured the world. Hartford didn't lack variety in his efforts to support the arts.

Hartford was an authority on handwriting analysis and accumulated an extensive library. When he interviewed a candidate to work for him, the candidate had to write a certain passage, which he then reviewed for signs of intelligence and character. Somehow, I passed this test. Over the years, he taught me some of the basics. He had done some interesting research. He commissioned someone to find writings of a dozen very famous or infamous people including Hitler, Napoleon and Einstein. The handwriting was compared for similarities or dissimilarities, and some knowledge was gained from that. He also was an underwriter of the research of an Austrian physician who had spent twenty years on the premise that, as a person develops cancer, the handwriting might show some sign of the disease which would help in making a correct prognosis. He did extensive testing with the cooperation of hospitals and doctors. It turns out that he had indeed identified some consistent changes in the handwriting of these people and found that the changes took place at an early stage. When his findings were tested, he had about 95% accuracy in forecasting certain types of cancer. This was deemed not good enough. For patients who had no other symptoms of having cancer, to tell them that they had cancer from the study of their handwriting did not seem to be appropriate.

Hartford was also interested in improving traffic flow in Manhattan. He pursued the idea that every other cross street should have a bridge over the East River with a major artery on the Queens and Brooklyn side for traveling north and south. This way, the traffic flow would be greatly relieved and the area on the east side of the river could be used more productively. He had an architect draw up the plan and unsuccessfully tried to convince city government and leading citizens to seriously assess the idea.

I had some exposure to the politics of New York. It is stranger than fiction. The stakes are so high, the concentration of power and wealth are so staggering that any project can be accepted or rejected as a result of luck, influence and negotiating skills. One small example was the fund raising Hartford did for a well-known senator. I was put in charge of collecting donations at a major fund raising party. In those days, there were already some laws which set down requirements for donors. One rule was that a union member could only donate from his personal funds and not from union money. During one fund-raising party, a burly type arrived on the scene. He obviously was a well-known figure as many people at the party came to say hello to him. When he came over to my table and presented me with a substantial check, I noted that it was a union check. I told him that I understood that we could not accept union funds. He laughed and said, "Sonny, if you know what is good for you, you better accept it. I will write a check to the union when I get back to the office". I was convinced that he had no intention of doing so. After a quick consultation with a political expert, I was told to accept the check, and somebody else would straighten it out. I didn't really believe this, but there was nothing I could do.

Hartford donated substantially to various politicians, but seemed to select the person rather than the party. He supported Nixon since his on and off again friend, Jim Crosby, was a major fund raiser for the Republican Party. After Nixon was elected, he personally wrote letters to Hartford. One letter outlined some of his views about the economy and asked for Hartford's opinion. Hartford was not too careful with his mail. He would read it and then drop it wherever he happened to be. Six weeks later, he found the letter and sent it to my office for me to draft a reply. I told him that it was a little embarrassing to answer the president of the United States in such a slow fashion. Nevertheless, he insisted on a draft. I assumed that Nixon was really not interested in Hunt's answer and that he probably wrote the letter to him to keep Hunt interested in him so that he would continue to donate money. I drafted an answer which I believed solved the dilemma. The letter stated that we didn't want to give the president a quick reply as we wanted to do our own research about some of the economic problems before we gave an answer. Hartford liked the draft, and it was sent. We never heard from Nixon in return.

One of the pleasures of my job was that I met a lot of people who ordinarily one would never meet, but only read about. One interesting man was Ted Sorensen, who had been one of the speech writers and leading advisers to President Kennedy. He gave good advice to Hartford. Lots of film or stage celebrities also came to visit him.

Another interesting venture for Hartford was the development of an oil shale industry in the US. Many projections showed that the world would soon run out of oil. The US has a fantastic amount of oil stored in shale in the Colorado area that could keep us in oil for a couple of centuries. The challenge was how to get it out of the stone at a competitive cost. Hartford helped a Swedish engineer who had a patent for a process that seemed like a breakthrough at obtaining oil at a reasonable price. He invested in an oil company which is now known as the Tosco Oil Shale Company. However, it proved to be a much more complicated and expensive undertaking than originally estimated. The price of conventionally extracted oil also had a great bearing on whether our government would support the long term effort. The company had some excellent people and was close to success. However, then the oil prices fell again and our government withdrew its support in the effort. Tosco decided to branch out into the conventional oil business, and Hartford lost interest.

When I started to work for Hartford, I talked to a senior partner of one of the main investment houses that handled his investments. Hartford's lawyers had done a very smart thing. When Hartford inherited his vast fortune, they took a substantial amount and set it up as a trust. Hartford could only draw on the income and not on the principal. This guaranteed that Hartford would never be a poor man, even if he lost all his other millions. However, I found out that nobody had ever investigated Hartford's personal business enterprises. They assumed that, with all the millions he had, he was in a high tax bracket. This was far from the truth. The trust was invested mostly in tax free bonds. When I told him that Hartford had so many business losses that he didn't pay any taxes and, therefore, his other assets did not have to be in tax free bonds, they were flabbergasted. This was one of my few claims to fame as a 3 % or 4% difference by switching to taxable bonds produced a tremendous increase in his personal income. Many times, I read the criticism that it is scandalous that some rich people do not pay any income taxes. What critics do not understand is that these people most often do not cheat, but have lost so much money in their business ventures that there is no income to pay tax on. This was certainly true in Hartford's case. I talked with him about that. He said, "Jim, don't think so 'middle income class!' I want to use my money as I see fit, and I really don't care whether I make money or not. I want to enjoy my life by pursuing the things that interest me." He always gave as an example the life of his sister who invested all her money with various well-known investment houses and accumulated even more wealth, but didn't do anything exciting or special with it.

Hartford lived in such a different world that it took me a long time to understand some of his motivations and quirks. One of his long-time employees told me that once he and Hartford were driving in Germany and got lost. They were near a railroad track, and Hunt suggested that they drive on the railroad track as he was sure that the track would lead them to the town they looking for. Hunt can be very persuasive, so they started to drive on the track. Soon they saw a train coming in their direction, but Hunt refused to get off the track explaining that the train would stop and then they could get better directions. The train did stop without killing them, and the engineer came toward them screaming in German. At that point, Hartford made his famous remark, "See! Typical German! All they can do is scream".

I was told that, during the war, Hunt was assigned as a Coast Guard skipper in the Pacific. His ship could have been a part of McHale's

Navy. He had a wine cellar on board and a couple of motorcycles for fast dates.

Some rich people seem to have some peculiar traits. When Hunt was living in the Bahamas, he would call his secretary in New York to call his Bahamian neighbor in the house next door to invite him for a drink. I could never find out whether he was too lazy to look up the telephone number or he didn't want to go through the effort to call his neighbor.

Hunt had a friend Chris who lived in Chicago. He had Greek heritage and played a leading role in trying to reinstall the royal house of Greece. He was a very wealthy man and was also very much involved in various cultural and artistic endeavors. We became good friends. One day, he called me and invited me to go with him to China. This was at the time that Kissinger and Nixon had reestablished a rapport with China. Our state department had invited thirty people to visit China and my friend was one of them. He had heard that there were still some openings, and he had proposed that I go along. All the people invited were asked to bring something especially American with them for a people to people visit with the Chinese. I decided to write some music to a favorite poem of Mao Tse Tung. My Presbyterian Church choir sang and recorded it. Because of some political event, the Chinese then restricted the number of Americans for the trip to twenty. I gave my cassette to Chris as I was eliminated from the trip. When he returned from China, he told me that, at a reception given by Mao, he had presented my cassette to him, and they had played it.

My final episode with Hunt was dealing with the Huntington Hartford Cultural Center in New York. Hunt had a good feel for collecting art, especially paintings that increased in value. He had quite a collection and concentrated on nineteenth century paintings. I believe that he helped to bring Salvador Dali to fame. He had quite a collection before I worked for him. Hunt decided to build a museum that would house his collection and have innovative exhibitions. With the help of Durrell Stone, one of the top architects in the country, he built the museum on Columbus Circle in New York City. It was a gem of a building. It was practically hand-made with imported marble and specially designed elevators. Unfortunately, no attention was given to the commercial aspect of the enterprise. The building was too small for major exhibitions, and it could handle a limited amount of traffic. On the top floor, it had a Polynesian restaurant with a breathtaking view of Central Park. Hunt had to subsidize the place with about a million a year. He tried to raise money with fundraisers, but with no success. . The common attitude was that he had built a monument to himself and that, since he was rich, why should anybody else support it. He had very artistically successful exhibitions, but there was no hope to break even. When I was helping to see what we could do financially, it became clear that we could reduce the cost somewhat, but that there was no way to make it financially viable. It took a long time to convince Hunt of that fact. He finally agreed that he could no longer afford to keep the building. He also had to sell some of his paintings to support his other ventures.

One night he called me and said that he had a great idea. He called me many times at night to tell me about some new idea, and my main job was to talk him out of it. However, this time he had an interesting idea. He had read about a Dr. Peter Sammartino who was the Chancellor of Fairleigh Dickinson University. He was given credit for being one of the country's top innovators in higher education. Hunt proposed that he would donate the museum to the university. In return, they had to keep the building for what it was intended. Hartford was very spontaneous and enthusiastic about his ideas. He immediately called Dr. Sammartino in London where it was the middle of the night. He was able to get Sammartino interested enough to have him come to New York and discuss the proposal. After our conversation, Peter needed to talk with his trustees. After that, we met with Mr. Fairleigh Dickinson, who was very excited about the project and promised to give an annual gift to make the venture viable. It was felt that the university would greatly benefit from a New York presence and that the faculty would surely support the venture. It should be noted that the Hudson River divides New York and New Jersey into two distinct cultures with very little overlapping, especially in society circles. The negotiations lasted a year. Hunt wanted to be sure that the deal was iron clad and there was no way for the university to keep the building for a few years and then sell it. Hunt finally agreed that, for every six years they kept the building, the university would get three million dollars from his estate with a maximum to twelve years. Dickinson was put on the board of the museum, and Peter Sammartino was to be the director. He had studied the operation and felt that he could make major improvements and reduce the cost. After we had concluded the very complicated agreement, Dickinson told me that any time I wanted to quit the Hartford enterprise, I should call him as he wanted me to work for his company, Becton Dickinson. Later on, when I decided to leave Hartford as my usefulness to him had diminished and my working hours were exhausting, I called Dickinson and he kept his promise, and I was hired as the head of the internal auditing staff.

Meanwhile, my own private life was in shambles. My wife continued to be an extremely difficult challenge. Although she had regular treatment from a psychiatrist, she was barely functional. She had taken a job at Sears as a stock clerk. She was offered the job of a sales clerk, but she was deathly afraid of the billing machine, and therefore didn't want the job. Our children were doing all right. However, my teenage daughter was very popular and attractive and had a choice of boyfriends who did not meet my minimum standards. Therefore, many arguments and teenage complications became the rule. With my two hour commute each way and many extra hours on the job, I was really fortunate that our kids did so well. In addition, almost every Sunday, I traveled an hour each way to the state institution in Totowa to see our daughter Nancy and preside over the parents group. Since I had also kept up my responsibilities in the church and on the school board, I had my hands full. During the latter part of my days working for Hartford, he rented an apartment for me in New York for the late nights when I had to attend a function. During that period, I felt very lonely and anxious. I met a divorced woman who was very appealing. She was well-known in the political arena and in society. We dated, and she pushed me toward a divorce from my wife. She did help me through a very difficult time. However, when it became time to make a decision, I decided that I would feel too guilty. I would feel like I was abandoning my responsibilities and especially my children. I called her and said that I could not do it. I was in my New York apartment at the time. Early the next day, I got a call from her teenage son who told me that his mother had tried to commit suicide and was in a hospital. I went to see her. She was quite sedated, but seemed to be recovering. Her son was also there. He held me responsible and threatened me. I visited her regularly, and the son calmed down as his mother told him that I was not to blame. She was Catholic and had been close to a priest whose judgment she really respected. He convinced her that she had some real problems and could not blame what she had done on me. Fortunately, she accepted that, and we separated on good terms. I felt very relieved and sure that I had done the right thing, especially with respect to my children. I could not bear the idea that my wife might be given responsibility for them as she was totally incapable. I found more and more that my children were everything to me.

My five years with Hartford were very interesting and gave me that rare opportunity to see how one percent of our population lives. Hartford was fortunate to have a very loyal and bright staff. His personal secretary had to keep track of all his appointments, turn people away in a diplomatic way when that was appropriate, and handle the constant emergencies that Hartford created by changing his mind about anything and everything. He was still destined to lose in a society where so many will try almost anything to have some of his money come their way and where the quality and ethical aspects of a venture play a secondary role to making a profit.

An aftermath of my Hartford days was my resolution to deal with the Hartford Cultural Center. When I joined Becton Dickinson, I told Dick Dickinson that I had serious doubts about whether the deficit of the cultural center could be reduced substantially. He had hopes that, with the effort of Peter Sammartino, that could be done. Peter worked very hard toward that end and was quite innovative. I was on the Board of Trustees of the cultural center, and Peter had added some very prominent people to the board. They all tried to help. Dickinson kept his promise but, after a few years, it became clear that the center would continue to have about a million dollar deficit a year. After many discussions, a most creative solution was found. Obviously, the university didn't want to lose the millions that would come from the Hartford estate if the building continued to be used non-commercially. One of the board members was the head of the Gulf and Western Corporation, which had their headquarters right on Columbus Circle. He proposed that the cultural center be donated to New York City, and the Gulf & Western Foundation would underwrite the maintenance of the building. That would be good public relations for Gulf and

Western and the city would get a beautiful facility. That is exactly what happened. The city has been using it as a tourist information center and to host exhibitions, and Hartford was more than satisfied with the new arrangement.

BECTON DICKINSON

In 1973, I started my new job as head of internal auditing of B&D. The company had been started by Fairleigh Dickinson, the father of Dick Dickinson, and Henry Becton. They were both traveling salesmen who met one day in a bar. Both wanted to get away from a traveling job. They were both in the same field. I believe they sold syringes and needles. They started their own company and were extremely successful. Later on, Dick Dickinson took over the management, while Mr. Becton played the role of goodwill ambassador for the company. Under Dick's leadership, the company flourished and expanded. One of their greatest successes was the development of the vacutainer system, which is well recognized as a major improvement in collecting blood from patients. When I joined the company, it had grown into a major entity. It had sales of about four hundred million dollars and had plants all over the US and in Mexico as well as ventures in Europe. It seemed to have an able management and had acquired a diverse group of companies that supplemented their products. One well-known product was the Ace bandage. In the seventies, the company produced about forty thousand different items.

Though I was really more interested in general management, I felt that, as an auditor, I had a unique chance to learn the major components of the company. The company was highly decentralized, and there were very few people in the company who had a good overview. I soon found out that the company had only given lip service to their audit department. The company had consistently grown since World War II. When Dickinson wanted to arrange some financing and could not get it, he decided that the company should build up a cash reserve so they would not need outside financing. In those days, the threat of takeovers stimulated by surplus cash was not usual.

The company reflected Dickinson's humanitarian lifestyle. Most employees stayed with the company for a lifetime and were proud to be part of it. High quality was a basic concept that was strictly adhered to. The company was still in the early stages of going truly international, and I detected the common aversion of Americans to venture abroad. They did set up an impressive headquarters for Europe in Grenoble, France. I reported to the company treasurer, a man of strong opinions, who had Dickinson's full confidence. He actually made the decision to hire me into his department. When I was originally interviewed, it was not very clear what I was going to do. The company treasurer had a temperament that, if he didn't like you or if you did something he didn't approve of, he left no doubt as to where he stood. He almost had an obsession about the various petty cash funds that were maintained in various departments. We checked them regularly, and there was big trouble if they didn't balance. I knew that he also kept his own fund. After I had been there long enough and had built a good relationship, I told him that I was going to have a surprise audit of his petty cash. He was not receptive to that idea as he felt the treasurer should be above that sort of thing. I insisted, as our outside auditors would find it peculiar that he had never been audited. He finally agreed. The next day, I did the audit and found that he never really kept a formal accounting. However, there was no evidence that he had short-changed the company. I wrote up a report recommending that he should follow the prescribed procedures of the company. To my surprise, he complimented me on my courage for following through. He felt that I was one of the few who were not afraid to stand up to him.

An internal audit should be a productive undertaking. It should not only test whether company procedures were followed, but it should recommend improvements that were either common sense or new ideas that had been successfully implemented at other locations. I was allowed to expand my staff. I also insisted that I should report directly to the finance committee of the board so that my department had maximum independence. I enjoyed building my department to a professional level and had some good people to work with.

After two years, I was asked to become the general manager of a new division called AAA. This division was responsible for developing markets in the Middle East, Africa, Australia, New Zealand and Asia. B&D had already established some business in these areas especially in Iran, South Africa, Australia and New Zealand. They accomplished this by having agreements with local distributors in those countries. There were some well-trained salesmen in AAA who had been visiting these distributors. I also had a good support staff and was able to add some more capable staff to our group. Our first task was to develop a plan. We looked at some 150 countries, some of which we had never heard of previously.

The responsibility of developing the overseas markets meant a lot of traveling. We had sorted out our priorities, and the main countries we wanted to concentrate on were: Greece, Turkey, Israel, Iran, Kuwait, Saudi Arabia, Egypt, Nigeria, South Africa, the Philippines, Australia, New Zealand and Thailand. We established offices in Athens with a regional manager responsible for the Middle East. The person we hired turned out to be invaluable. Alberto was born in Alexandria, Egypt and had a Greek father and an Italian mother. He had a French wife and had previously worked for an American company. He spoke fluent Egyptian, Greek, Italian, French and English. In his previous jobs, he had traveled extensively in the Middle East and had a good understanding of cultural differences. We had many planning meetings with him to begin to understand the local culture in these countries. We had a challenging task. It was essential that we understand the level of medical services in each country as we could only sell instruments that would fit in with the country's present protocol.

A good example was Turkey. Because Turkey is a very poor country, they used reusable needles. The pharmacist, not the doctor, gave injections. If we didn't know this, we would be trying to sell our needle to the wrong party. Also, the pharmacist did not practice according to our rules. A reusable needle becomes dull after 4 or 5 uses. However, the Turkish pharmacists used a needle more than ten times, at which time you had to practically use a hammer to get the needle through the skin. We talked to the pharmacists, and they explained that their profit margin was not enough to allow them to use the needle only five times. To our horror, we also discovered that, after each use, they put the needle in boiling water, but they didn't keep it in long enough to sterilize the needle. We knew that there had been various epidemics in Turkey, but the government had attempted to keep them secret. A further problem was the maze of people we were supposed to bribe to have our product imported. At that time, American companies were not allowed to bribe anybody. We solved this problem by selling our product to a Turkish firm who, in turn, would bribe the proper officials. The result, of course, was that the Turks had to pay even more, as the middleman would want to make a profit. The product probably would cost a lot less than if we could have sold it directly. We did try to work very hard with governments to educate them in how to gradually improve the quality of medicine. It posed an interesting problem for us. We had basically developed a product for the sophisticated level of medicine in the US. The developing nations or the underdeveloped nations could not afford our products. In addition, our products actually didn't really fit into their way of practicing medicine. We gave some serious thought to developing products that would be of practical use in their medical systems, but didn't end up doing this. We probably still export a lot of products that are of little use to these countries.

Besides learning about our own products, I tried to become familiar with my clientele. Alberto took me on an orientation tour to teach me some of the dos and don'ts. You cannot go to Israel first and then to Saudi Arabia as your passport would have an Israeli stamp on it and then the Saudis would not admit you. You, therefore, needed either two passports or a loose leaf insert. The same principle also applies to South Africa and Nigeria. In Iran during the reign of the Shah, the country was very western oriented. However, the culture was very different from our culture. You had to learn patience and take part in endless negotiations. To teach me this lesson, Alberto took me to a bazaar in Egypt. We were going to buy some perfume. Families of the merchants in these bazaars dated back for centuries. The particular stall that we went to had a New York Times article pinned on the wall which described the family heritage. We were greeted by the owner who embraced Alberto like a long lost friend. He asked about his family and then we were offered tea. Egyptian tea is just sugar with a little tea added. After our tea, I had to describe my wife's personality. This was all necessary, he explained, so that he could mix the right ingredients to make the perfect perfume for my wife. He then offered us an aphrodisiac. After all this, he mixed various essences, and I had to make the final selection. Alberto had warned me that I should not participate in the price negotiations. He would show me how that was done. Alberto asked the man how much he wanted for the perfume. The vendor asked for a hundred dollars, which I thought was not unreasonable for the quantity and the custom made perfume. However, when he said one hundred dollars, Alberto got up and told me that we were leaving. He said that he had never been so insulted. He thought he was a friend of the perfumer and then to ask a price that was an embarrassment in front of Alberto's boss was too much. The man started to expound on all the costs he had and his need to support a large family. Half an hour later, we settled on $25. I had lost my patience and told Alberto that I thought that amount was extremely reasonable. Alberto told me later that, if I had kept my mouth shut, he would have gotten it down to $16. He explained that haggling was a way of life and probably the greatest entertainment for these merchants. They really looked down on Americans as they didn't understand and didn't negotiate.

In Iran, I was told the people were very formal, and usually you were not invited to their homes. If you were invited, you should consider that a real measure of friendship–almost like becoming a member of the family. I became good friends with our main distributor in Iran. He came from a very prominent family and had gone to an American university. The first time I went to his house for dinner, I wanted to tell him how beautiful his house was. I was especially impressed with a particular painting. When I was ready to leave, the family presented me with the painting. Alberto had not told me that their hospitality was such that, if you expressed a great liking for anything in their house, they were tradition bound to give it to you. I don't remember how I convinced them that I didn't want to take it from them, but we remained good friends. One consistent truth seemed to hold–if you shook hands on a deal, you could be assured that they would honor the agreement. Nevertheless, because the Shah's government was so corrupt, it was no surprise that Iran fell apart.

Saudi customs provided me with another lesson. Drinking alcohol was not allowed. Yet the Saudis would get whisky on the black market at an exorbitant price to please their American friends. If they were caught, they would be thrown in jail. Alberto had devised a clever antidote. He asked his doctor to give him a letter which stated that he had a rare disease and was not allowed to drink any type of alcoholic beverage. I obtained a similar letter. In Saudi Arabia, each office had a large photo of the king and one of his brothers. Nobody seemed to know who had the real power so, to play it safe, they hung both pictures. On one of my trips to Saudi Arabia, I stayed in a sort of motel. The motel had a large room that looked like a classroom. Alberto said that it was really a disguised movie theatre. Since it was illegal to show movies, they did so in this underground fashion. Another time I was buying a watch and, all of a sudden, the salesman jumped over the counter and, together with some other personnel, yelled at a customer. A knife was drawn, and the customer was pushed out of the door. The salesman explained that he hated Palestinians as they were arrogant and acted like they wanted to take over the country. This particular customer was rude to one of their salesmen, so he decided to throw him out of the store. The whole incident was frightening.

My acquaintance with a real sheik provided other interesting insights. He was a young man in his late twenties and was fabulously wealthy. He had a fleet of cars parked strategically throughout the town so that, if one car broke down, he could easily get to another. He also had a fleet of helicopters to use if the streets were inaccessible. One night, he treated me to dinner in a restaurant. For the occasion, he had hired a band that he was told could play American music. That proved to be partly correct. They were able to play Happy Birthday which they ended up playing all night. I asked my host whether he traveled much. He replied that he was a sheik and explained that his tribe really had a Jewish heritage, but centuries ago had turned to the Muslim religion. He said that, for eleven months, he practiced his religion and, for one month, he would take his vacation in Egypt and live like a westerner. This meant that he had girls and drank and lived the high life. He didn't see anything controversial in this. He saw it as an antidote to his normal lifestyle. The wealth of these families was expressed in billions of dollars. They struggled to grow from a very restricted lifestyle dominated by their religious and cultural heritage to a western lifestyle incorporating its best and worst characteristics.

One strong characteristic of the Saudi heritage was their hospitality.

The owner of one of the main distributors we dealt with always insisted on meeting me personally at the airport. Usually the planes arrived hours late. One time, I found him asleep on a bench at the airport when my plane arrived at about 2:00 in the morning, instead of 11:00 at night. We usually stayed in the Sheraton Hotel in Teheran. There were not many hotels to choose from, and this was considered the place where officials like me should stay. The problem was that the hotel was owned by the Shah. When he had friends or acquaintances coming, he would kick out any guests at the hotel. I found out that my friend had bribed the desk clerks with substantial money to protect me and others from being thrown out. He never mentioned it to me because that was his idea of being a good friend. The hotel was beautiful, and the service was good.

Once, I came with my senior sales manager. He looked like an All American football player. I had told him that, if he wanted to stay in my good graces, he should bring his tennis racket. I always took my tennis gear wherever I went. Once I played in Italy at the tennis court of a nice hotel. However, there were chickens walking around on the court. I was not used to that, and I asked the hotel manager to do something about it. He said that was not possible as he was on good terms with his neighbor who was a chicken farmer. He said the chickens had been on the court ever since he could remember and were experienced in avoiding the balls. This time at the Sheraton Hotel in Teheran, I planned to play at 6:00 p.m. with my associate. It soon started to become dark. We noticed that there were floodlights on the court. I went to see the manager, and he came with me to turn the lights on. When he saw my friend, he said, "We have a problem". The hotel rules specified that players had to be dressed in white, and my colleague was not. I said, "Well then you have a problem". I asked him if he was familiar with American football, and he said that he was. I said, "Have a good look at my friend. He is six foot three and weighs over 200 pounds". I said that he was a well-known football player, and I was afraid to tell him that we could not play. I suggested that the manager tell him. He was a man of small proportion and immediately appreciated what I was saying. He said, "Well, this is a special situation, and I will make an exception". When traveling abroad, one has to be inventive.

Our efforts in our new venture started to pay off. Over the three years that I was in charge, we had gone from a few millions to a fifteen million sales volume. My trips were exhausting as I had to represent the home office and, therefore, had to act and look the part. One of my regular rounds was to fly from New York to South Africa, stay there for three days, then go on to Australia and New Zealand for a week, and then go home. Often, when I arrived in Johannesburg in the afternoon, I had to attend a dinner that same night. Frequently, the guests were government officials and the partners of the distributorship we had an exclusive contract with. South Africaners were very outspoken and felt that we Americans were hypocrites telling others how to live without practicing what we preached in our own lives. It always became a lively conversation. Our distributor had an enlightened outlook on the racial problem. They had hired blacks years ago and had promoted them on merit the same as they would do for their white employees. Their senior manager was black. This was unusual. However, sadly, the blacks still had to commute to their black townships and endure many of the insults of racism. I had concluded that the principles developed by Mr. Sullivan, known as the Sullivan Rules, made sense. Our primitive approach of using sanctions always hurt the wrong people, even though they might work in the long term. But, at what cost to many of the population who were not involved in making the racial rules–especially in South Africa where the poor blacks took the brunt of the suffering because of the sanctions. We still applied the same methods in the nineties. It is hard to believe that we could not be more creative in our foreign policies.

I loved South Africa as a country. The climate was like California. It was unspoiled, and the individuals that I dealt with were refreshing. Unfortunately, because of the slave labor exploitation, everything was kept in meticulous condition. The gardens were gorgeous, especially in Capetown, and everything was clean.

I also enjoyed Australia and New Zealand where just about everybody is a sports fan. For main sporting events, most businesses would close so that everybody could watch. In both countries, we were well represented. The owner of the distributorship in Melbourne was a typical Australian. He had been a car racer before he started a medical instrument business and did well in both areas. The distributor in New

Zealand was also an interesting fellow. He was married to a woman from Finland and had two nice young children. They would show me around Auckland, and that was always a joy. Auckland is beautiful. You have the mountains and the ocean and a nice climate. I once walked along the bay and was impressed with the beautiful yachts. I talked to one man whose boat had a Dutch flag. He told me his life's story. He had been a successful businessman in Holland, had never married and, one year, took a vacation trip to New Zealand. He liked it so much, especially the sailing, that he never returned to Holland. He called his lawyer and told him to sell everything he owned, including his business, as he was going to live in New Zealand. That had happened about ten years ago, and he had not regretted it. Another trip was to a swimming area that consisted of three pools fed by three different geysers. One kept the water at 60 degrees, one at 70 degrees and one at 80 degrees. It was an interesting experiment to decide in which pool to start. I went to a Presbyterian church one Sunday, and the minister announced that their new Bibles, "Good News for Modern Man", had arrived. In New Jersey, we had been using these Bibles for at least ten years. This confirmed my main observation about New Zealand. The good news is that it is so far from Europe and the US that their people do not have to get caught up with some of the problems that we have, such as our racial problems. The bad news is that there is a considerable time lag for new ideas to reach them. I loved it nevertheless.

I found traveling in Africa an endurance test. Plane schedules were not adhered to, reservations were not necessarily honored, and usually the passengers brought everything that they owned with them on the plane, thereby crowding the plane to a dangerous and uncomfortable level. My first trip to Lagos was a memorable experience. I had made the mistake to go first to South Africa and then to Nigeria. When I arrived at Lagos, the custom officer told me to wait. After quite a wait, a boy of about fourteen years of age came over and told me that I probably had a serious problem. He asked me if I had come from South Africa and I said yes. He explained that the customs person had noted that in my passport and now would make life difficult for me. He said that, if I gave him twenty dollars, he would talk to the customs officer and solve my problem. I decided to try it. Sure enough, in about half and hour, I was called by the officer. He told me that I had not had all the necessary vaccines. I didn't argue, and then he interrogated me for some time about my company and where they did business. He finally let me go through, but he instructed me that I had to get the missing vaccine. Otherwise, I could not leave the country. I then went to the taxi stand where I found my young friend waiting for me. He told me that the next problem was to find a taxi that was willing to drive me to town as it was quite late. He asked for another tip, and he got me a taxi. The driver was a huge man in flowing robes. He drove me to the hotel and, when we arrived, he told me that he could not accept dollars. Passengers must pay in local currency. I told him to wait, and I would change dollars in the hotel. He said that was not possible as the cashier window in the hotel was closed. He then told me he would accept US money, but I had to pay him another twenty dollars for the risk he took. He was too big for me to fight, and I paid his fee. The next morning, I talked to the hotel manager and explained what had happened. He was furious and insisted that I go with him to the taxi stand and point out the driver. He said he had a good idea who he was because he was always stationed at this stand and had pulled that trick before. I was a little concerned about my health and safety, but I am also a sucker for fair play, so I went with him. The driver was there and then the manager took over. They argued fiercely, but I got my money back. Now, I had to worry about my vaccination. I called the US Embassy, and they told me to ignore the vaccinations as the medical practice was so bad that I might die from a needle infection. However, I did go the government's health office, and they told me that they could give me the vaccine injection. When I saw how the doctor did this, I realized the danger. As in Turkey, he would use reusable needles without proper sterilization. When it was my turn, I told the doctor that I would be glad to pay for a fresh needle, and he accepted my offer.

When I finished my business in Lagos, I had some time in the morning before returning to the airport. I sat at the bar and talked to a man from Texas. He asked me, at some point, when my flight was leaving. It was 11 a.m. at the time, and I told him I was leaving around 3 p.m. He said, "You had better run if you want to make it!" When I had arrived in Lagos, it was the middle of the night, and the trip to the hotel took about twenty minutes. Now, I found that, in the middle of the day, nothing moved. All kinds of merchants were lined up along the roads selling everything from cloth to radios to carpets. I barely made it in time. However, when I arrived, there was no sign of a plane or attendants. I was to fly to Cairo on Middle East Airlines. I just waited and more people arrived and, all of a sudden, a counter official arrived. People had placed their luggage strategically in the middle of the room so they could move fast in any direction. The reason for that was that reservations didn't mean much. Whether you got on the plane was governed more by who was there first. I lined up and, all of a sudden, an Egyptian Admiral showed up in uniform. He pushed everybody aside to be first in line. At this point, I was so angry that I stopped him and told him that he had no right to push everybody aside and I would not stand for it. The man was flabbergasted, but then resumed his push. I was then quickly rescued by an airline official, and she assured me that I would get a seat on the plane. I consider myself an experienced traveler but, once in a while, I let my principles interfere with my better judgment. In this case, it paid off.

In Egypt, you also have to adjust to their way of doing things. My regional manager had told me that I should not get a visa in New York for Egypt. He would handle it when I arrived there. I didn't really like this idea and went to the Egyptian embassy to obtain the visa. When my plane arrived at Cairo Airport, I could see a big limousine driving toward the area where our plane would park. When I disembarked from the plane, my manager Alberto was waiting. Like some important person, I got in the car which then drove to a separate customs facility used for VIPs who apparently give generous tips for the special treatment. When I told Alberto that I had already obtained a visa, he was quite upset. Instead of moving right through the process, I had to stand in line and go through the regular customs procedure. These employees were not bribed and took their time handling the large crowd. It took an hour to get through customs. Now we had to wait for the luggage. Alberto had a solution for that. He paid one of the porters an extra fee, and he took us behind the scenes where they were bringing in the wagons with the luggage. We were able to take our luggage directly from the wagon and leave without going through luggage inspection. In the Middle East, when you departed on a flight, they would assemble all the luggage right next to the plane, and then you had to point out which pieces were yours. They then would load it on board. The theory was that if you were willing to have that luggage put on the plane you were flying in, the luggage could not contain a bomb. The problem was that nobody had told me about this procedure. The first trip that I took in the Middle East, I was lucky enough to look out the window and see my luggage standing there. I thought that was peculiar and asked the stewardess why my luggage was there. She explained, and I was able to leave the plane and identify my luggage.

Egypt is a beautiful country. I especially enjoyed it because the wife of our manager in Cairo was a professor in Egyptian antiquity. She would take a day off to spend with me. We went to the museum in Cairo, which has an unbelievable number of ancient artifacts. It is almost indescribable. We also went by horse and buggy to explore the Sahara desert. Once, we had to crawl through a narrow tunnel to get into a cave which contained the belongings of a physician who was famous during the reign of the Pharaohs. Inscriptions describing his life were engraved on the walls, and my friend would explain what they said. It was fascinating. You really stand in awe of that long ago culture.

The president of our distributor in Cairo always used the occasion of my visits to show me the Egyptian nightlife. He took me to a nightclub which was housed in a tent in the desert. He explained that his wife didn't approve of going to these kinds of places, so he used me as an excuse to go. Egyptians are in general very educated and artistic people. Cairo has an enormous number of nightclubs where actors appear together with singers, bands, magicians, and so on. Groups of performers would contract with the various nightclubs so that one group would entertain, for example, from 9 p.m. to 10 p.m. and then the next group would arrive. Since I didn't speak the Arabic language, I missed a lot. What were fascinating to me were the belly dancers. Belly dancing is a highly developed art in the Middle East. I saw one dancer put a cane on top of her bosom and shake her whole body without losing the cane. Of course, she was well endowed by nature. My problem was that my host wanted to see the whole series of shows. They started at about 10:00 p.m. and would go on until about 6:00 a.m. On top of that, since it was his big night, he would order several bottles of whisky which was his favored drink. He assumed that he did me a favor as well since all Americans are assumed to love whiskey. By twelve o'clock, I had had enough, but I was not able to politely convince him that it was time to go home. He scared me a little when he said that there was so much poverty in Egypt that it was not unusual to be robbed. He told me not to worry, because he was hiding a revolver in his jacket. I asked him if he ever had used it. He said yes as he had been a military man. Those evenings were exhausting. Because of the warm climate, the custom in Egypt was to start work later in the morning, have a long lunch break with a siesta, and then work until eight o'clock. Dinner was normally eaten at ten o'clock.

Egypt was an important country for us partly because our government started to heavily subsidize the country and that subsidy included the medical field. Although highly educated, the country had not seen any prosperity for the general population. The poverty was appalling. On the outskirts of Cairo, I saw people living in dirt huts. There was not enough food, and many died from starvation. There was a small group of very wealthy people, but the rest of the population suffered. I once read somewhere that, to really assess the stability of a country, you had to study the size of the population that was poor or middle class or rich. The theory was that the poor didn't own anything and, therefore, didn't care about anything, but could be drawn to a demagogue politician who would promise a better future–someone like a Hitler or some fanatical religious leader who would promise the heavenly hereafter like the Islam fundamentalists. The rich had enough money to leave the country in case of problems. The middle class was the only group who gave stability as they had something to protect, but would not have enough riches to go to another country in case of trouble. The United States has a history of this kind of stability because of its large middle class.

Another country that I enjoyed very much was Thailand. There is so much culture in the world that we are never exposed to in the West. The Vietnamese have a military history on a par with the Prussian Germans. The Thais are considered to have an artistic heritage as impressive as Italy. Their temples and palaces are unique. Our distributor in Thailand was very proud of this heritage and would take me on many trips to see these beautiful places. Outside of Bangkok, we were often transported in large canoes with an outboard motor. The rivers and canals were so overcrowded and the boats went so fast that I felt like I was in New

York on 42nd Street during the rush hour. The disheartening part, once again, was the poverty of the people. I was caught once in Bangkok in a tropical rainstorm. Apparently, nobody could afford rubbers or boots. The drainage system was overtaxed, and soon the streets were flooded. Street vendors were selling plastic bags to put over shoes to keep them dry. It was quite a sight to see people shuffling along in that kind of footwear. This all happened in the seventies, so conditions may have changed since then.

During my three years as head of the AAA division, I was successful in building a bright and loyal group which was highly motivated. My main job was to protect them as the politics in most companies, especially at the top, are so unbelievable that it beats fiction. I reported to the International Vice President. He was a graduate of MIT and was very bright and knowledgeable, but extremely ambitious. He, in turn, reported to a Senior Vice President who had spent most of his career with the company, primarily as an international salesman. The Senior Vice President relied heavily on his Vice President, certainly with respect to day to day operations. My boss was a died-in-the-wool capitalist and defined success as making a profit. He was constantly at odds with my sales manager, who had also been with the company for most of his career. The sales manager suffered a lot from seeing himself as "God sent", and it was a challenge for me to bring him down to earth. He resented that I, a lowly accountant who didn't know much about the various products, was brought in as the head of the division. I tried to convince him that there was plenty of room for all of us to grow and that I would sincerely appreciate it if he could see me as a partner in the endeavor. I always thought of people who worked for me as partners and would give them a lot of freedom if they showed common sense and took their responsibilities seriously. Of course, as a manager, the main challenge is to motivate others to see it your way and to create an atmosphere that is conducive to growth of the individual. That means, in my opinion, that you create a friendly, competitive situation and appreciate your employees. I told them that anybody who had a problem could talk to me. I had an open door policy and always put openness at the top of my priorities. People are the most important assets of any company—not the machines or the money in the bank.

In our annual planning, we would get together with the senior management of the company, and those sessions were tough. In developing such a vast territory encompassing three continents, there were many choices to make, and the money allocated was extremely limited. On top of that, we had to deal with the various prima donnas who participated in the debate. Our meetings went from the sublime to the ridiculous to the nasty. Fortunately, I had created a loyal and hard working group who usually could effectively demonstrate the rationale for our annual proposals. We grew rapidly and gained some respect throughout the hierarchy. Fairleigh Dickinson took an interest in our efforts and gave us his full support.

Dickinson was planning for his gradual retirement and had chosen two employees to succeed him in the top job. One had an engineering background and the other was well versed in sales and finance. One day, I was called in by Mr. Dickinson. He was evaluating a company that produced specialty paper. They were not doing well and wanted to sell the company. Dickinson explained that Becton Dickinson's products were medical, but that the raw material for many products included plastics and special paper. Therefore, he thought it would be beneficial to buy a paper company which would cut out the middleman through which we normally bought paper. His two understudies disagreed. Since he felt that he and his understudies respected my know-how in assessing a business because of my background at Lybrand and because of my experience as a CPA, I should do an independent evaluation of the paper company. I did the evaluation. I reported that the purchase price was not cheap and that the company had lost a lot of its inherent strength, but that it still had good expertise in the making of specialized paper. I recommended that the company should go ahead with the purchase. What I didn't know was that Dickinson's two apprentices were dead set against it. Though I stuck to my conclusions, they didn't feel that the company should buy a company that was losing money.

A rift developed between Dickinson and his two chosen successors. They were trying to convince the board that Dickinson should retire now and become a Vice Chairman. Dickinson was still by far the largest stockholder in the company and, therefore, wielded a lot of power. The struggle became very bitter. Dickinson really had led the company to its phenomenal success in size, reputation and profitability.

The shock came when the board unexpectedly voted to have him resign as Chairman of the Board and be demoted to a secondary role. He was devastated. I would say that it almost cost him his life. You do not need a gun to kill someone. This kind of power play is not unusual in management. Although you often read articles about how people have successfully managed companies, you rarely hear about how these great corporate leaders have often eliminated their associates and sacrificed their families to get to the top.

Dickinson was now planning a counter attack. He contacted Salomon Brothers, a prominent Wall Street firm, and asked them to find a suitable buyer for his company stock and was looking to have this company also buy enough shares to have effective control. Salomon Brothers found an interested party, the Sun Oil Company. A number of banks were also holding Becton Dickinson stock in their portfolio. Salomon Brothers called these banks with a proposal to offer $45 per share. The shares were currently selling at about $26. They would call the following Thursday in the afternoon and wanted a yes or no answer from these banks. Only a few banks said that they couldn't do such a transaction on such short notice, because they had to reach the parties who actually owned the stock. Most of the banks said that they could make the decision. The following Thursday, Salomon Brothers bought enough stock to have a controlling interest for Sunoco. When the two understudies found out about this total surprise, they were able to marshal some senators in Washington and the SEC to investigate the legality of these moves. The affair became known as The Saturday Night Raid.

The reason why Sun Oil Company was interested in the deal was that they wanted to diversify, and Becton Dickinson was cash rich and had a solid reputation. Many times, companies never look much beyond the surface and buy for superficial reasons. The beauty of this marriage would have been that Sun Oil could supply plastics directly as they were in the oil business. Sun Oil also had experience in international operations, while Becton Dickinson was still in the early stages of development. Sun Oil also had very sophisticated management and computer systems which could be put to good use by Becton Dickinson. However, unfortunately, Salomon Brothers lost the case. I think that, if they had used more conventional methods, they probably would have been successful. Dickinson was also accused of illegal action in selling his shares to Sun Oil Company. However, he was vindicated and his sale went through.

Becton Dickinson ultimately overcame all the fighting at the top. When the internal fight within management took place, it was clear that all of Dickinson's friends would be scrutinized. I watched as various people disappeared through retirement.

I had made many friends at Becton Dickinson, and our group had worked well together. We had, meanwhile, moved to a leased space in a brand new facility in Paramus, NJ. The company had done a thorough job in looking at all aspects of the move. After checking the usual concerns such as transportation, accessibility, safety, accommodation within and outside the building, the only flaw that they had been unaware of was the existence of a building across the street that housed the criminally insane. We found out that, fairly regularly, people escaped.

I had not seen any signs that I was going to be discarded because of my relationship with Dickinson. I ended up lasting a year. We had negotiated a very large deal with a company in Eastern Europe which was supported by the local government. What we didn't know was that this company would smuggle their products into Western Europe and sell them below market value. I was held responsible for not foreseeing this. My day of reckoning had come. I had been with the company for five years and had enjoyed most of those years. It was sad that management had to go through all the power plays because the rank and file employees were good and productive people. Under Dickinson's leadership, the company had had high ethical standards and had treated their employees so well that most people stayed with the company for their whole career.

I was frankly tired from all the pressures and the extensive travel. However, it had also been exciting and a tremendous experience for me. Unfortunately, in those days, there were no laws to protect you from losing pension benefits. Although I did get a token pension from the company, I lost most of my benefits from my five years with Hart, Inc., my thirteen years with Hartford and my five years with Becton Dickinson. Because of the substantial medical bills for my wife and my daughter, saving had been extremely difficult. Money matters were further aggravated by my wife since she expressed her anger by spending money. I controlled the checkbook and, at one point, took all the credit cards away. I had protected our credit rating and had never defaulted on any bill. However, my wife often was clever enough to find ways to charge purchases. It was a losing battle. Fortunately, I was always able to provide well for my children, and they appreciated that fact even more when they married and found that making and managing money was really not that easy.

At the time of my leaving Becton Dickinson, my oldest daughter, Nancy, was still at the Totowa State Institution. My second daughter, Joyce, had graduated from high school and was not very interested in going to college. She did well at Sears and had a serious boyfriend, who also worked at Sears. After a lot of conversations, I finally convinced her that it would be good for her future to go to college. Our society seems to make two distinct class separations, one based on money and the other on whether or not you are a college graduate. Joyce was accepted at Mount Ida College which, at that time, was a two-year school. I drove her down to the school in Newton, MA. There were quite a lot of forms to fill out, so I offered to take her belongings to her room while she registered. She had more than a carload of things, and her room was on the second floor, down a long corridor. She got delayed in the registration process, and I kept carrying the endless flow of her necessities, including some furniture. After two hours, I was finished and sat down. I then realized that I could hardly get up as my back was very painful and stiff. My daughter had returned, and I insisted that, somehow, I was going to drive back to New Jersey. I did, with the major problem being able to put quarters in the numerous toll booths. I had to really toss the coins as my back was now rigid. I made it home and called our doctor. He came and suggested that I try to take hot baths and, otherwise, lay flat on my bed. I crawled to the bathtub and filled it with hot water. I then tried to get over the side into the tub. I realized that I could hardly move at all. We called the ambulance while I was lying on the bathroom floor. When the paramedics arrived, I told them that, because every move was so painful, I probably would pass out. Fortunately, the three paramedics were very experienced. They put me in a bed sheet and all three lifted me up so I didn't have to move at all. The specialist at the hospital told me that I had two discs in the lower back that had been damaged and surgery was necessary. In order to do the operation, they had to take measurements in great detail to have an exact reading of the damage. That process was unbelievable. They had to move my body into certain positions. I screamed, but finally three strong men, ignoring my screaming, got me twisted in the right positions. The operation was successful, but I had to remain in the hospital for two months. For some unknown reason, some patients can suffer from depression after this type of surgery. I was one of those patients. The pain was insufferable, and I couldn't sleep. They gave me powerful pills, but things got even worse. I finally asked them to call my wife's psychiatrist to see if he could give me some medicine that would relieve my depression, which just made me want to die. He came to see me and told me that he was going to perform a minor miracle. He said that the medicine that they had given me was out of date, but he was sure that he could help me. With the change in medication, the next day I was a changed man. I had lost strength in my muscles and had to learn to walk again. It took me about six months to recover from the ordeal. I will have to be careful for the rest of my life, but have had a few relapses, though nothing very serious.

BENNINGTON COLLEGE

I did some considerable thinking after I ended my stint at Becton Dickinson. I had not finalized just what to do. However, fate helped me along. Mr. Dickinson's wife was a graduate of Bennington College in Vermont. He was as devoted to her college as he was to his own college, Williams College. Accordingly, they supported each school financially on an equal basis. He also was very active in the management of the school. For years, he had been the head of the Finance Committee of the Board of Trustees. He called me and asked if I was interested in becoming the Financial Vice President of the school. I gathered information about the school and found that it was unique in many ways. In the twenties, a Reverend Booth was the pastor at the Congregational Church in Old Bennington, a community created by wealthy people from Troy, Albany, Boston and New York who had built summer homes in that town. Reverend Booth had two teenage daughters and was concerned that there was no appropriate high school in Bennington and, therefore, he would have to send them away to school. He talked to some leading families about financing a new private school. A group of local women liked the idea, but were more interested in starting a college for girls as they wanted to be pioneers in preparing women for careers. These women were very prominent, and they mustered the help of the presidents of Harvard and Smith to help in developing plans for a college. Years later, they had enough money to start a school in Bennington. The school was opened in the middle of the 1933 recession. I believe that the fee was $250, but no financial aid was available. They built temporary dormitories which are still in use today and are better built than the "permanent" buildings built since then.

The college has made a name for itself. They have attracted a brilliant group of scholars, especially in the visual and performing arts. In dance, the school had a close relationship with Martha Graham. Most of the early students came from well-connected wealthy families. Right from the start, the college advanced the idea of emancipation for women and set up an educational system based on the ideas of the educator John Dewey. Learning by doing was one of his principles and, consequently, each academic year, all students had to go out and work during January, February and March. Rumor had it that it was partly done to keep the utility costs down. Over the years, a system was developed that put actual control of the college in the hands of the faculty. Deans were chosen for a three-year term from among the faculty. The result was that the elected dean had to serve two masters, the president and the faculty. Since they would be returning to the faculty after their term was up, they were often not so interested in helping the president in the controversial cases where the faculty had a different opinion.

The college was not interested in fund raising, as they were worried that the contributors would have too much power. Because of this, they ran deficits which ordinarily would not be known until the college year was completed, as the bookkeeping system was rather primitive. When the deficits were discovered, somebody from the college would call an alumna and ask for a gift to cover the deficit. All this was possible as the college was very small in numbers. When enrollment started to increase and budgets became larger, some changes needed to be made. When I reviewed the financial situation in 1978, I discovered that the college was basically bankrupt. That inspired me to take on the job of restoring it to financial health. I told Dickinson that I was interested.

I was then interviewed by the president and chair of the board. The president was a brilliant scholar, born and raised in New York City, with very strong convictions about social justice. He had been the president of Queens College and was the only one who had stood against the politicians when they wanted to cut back on the budgets of the state schools. He had been at Bennington for three years to get the experience of a private liberal art school. However, he disliked living in a small town like Bennington and used every opportunity to get back to New York. He had little respect for most of the faculty as, over the years, they had become so entrenched that, in his opinion, they were not very productive since they lived on past glory. He had a biting sense of humor and was not afraid to speak his mind in the many stormy faculty meetings. He was close to a nervous breakdown when I met him. He said that he would give me carte blanche in running the business end of the college. I took an immediate liking to the man and was in awe of his intellectual capacity. He recommended me for the job.

I was then interviewed by the woman who was the chairperson of the board. She was a lovely woman, quite intelligent, but had no clue what was going on in the financial operation of the college. She confessed to me that she had been the chair for a long time, but had never understood the financial reports which were prepared by the auditors. She was too embarrassed to ask others at the college. She said that, if I could explain the latest financial report to her, I was hired. Fund accounting, in my opinion, was created to satisfy the lawyers and, therefore, is totally useless to the layman. I showed her that, if you extract from the report the items listed as cash, receivables, investments and inventory and, if you then subtract from that sum any items indicating a debt to an outside party, you have the basic net worth according to the books. She was astounded at the simplicity, but also shocked to see that the college was in such a bad state.

The college had one of the richest groups of alumnae in the country but, because of its policy not to raise money, there was no endowment. Prior to my arrival, the college had decided to build a state of the art Visual and Performing Arts Building. It was a marvel of a building with a dance facility that was so excellent that dance studios from New York came to use it. It had pieces of equipment that had never been used anywhere else, some of which didn't work. The Sculpture Building was another building that was always a success on a guided tour for parents and applicants. Although Mr. Dickinson and some others had made substantial gifts toward these facilities, it was by far not enough to pay for the construction. The school tried to run a capital campaign but, since they had no experience in fund raising, it never reached anywhere near the goal that had been set. The result was a debt that the college could ill afford. I told Dickinson that, if I assumed the responsibility, I saw him as a silent partner who would provide the absolutely necessary funds to keep the college alive. He was willing to help as much as he could.

The alumnae, one of the hidden assets of the college, had never been effectively used. I counted on their support. They would certainly be very embarrassed if the school, from which they had graduated, had to close its doors. At one of the board meetings, one trustee who was an alumna stated that, as long as she was on the board, there was no way that the college would go under. She was a very wealthy woman and would be able to create an instant endowment. However, there is a difference between talk and action, and it took more than seven years to see some meaningful fund raising results at Bennington.

Meanwhile, my family had moved into a very nice house on top of a hill with a beautiful view of the valley. It was on the outskirts of Bennington and, adjacent to our backyard, was the woods. I had never lived in such a rural environment, and I loved it. Every day, I enjoyed the view. Nature provided an ever-changing scene. Instead of fighting traffic and spending two hours commuting each way, I could get to work in about 15 minutes with no traffic jams. Prior to our move, we had to endure the oil crisis, which necessitated standing in line at 4:00 in the morning to get some gas. In Bennington, there was no gas shortage because, even though the tourists had stopped coming, they still had an allocation of fuel based on the tourist trade. The gas attendants even cleaned your windshield and checked the oil. When I came to Vermont, I thought that we would need long johns, but I never used them. A more useful acquisition was a large snow blower. I bought it second hand and did use it, even if it had the tendency to start easily only in the summer– not in the winter. My son finally found the solution after ten years–namely, a can of dry gas as an additive. I was used to the city lifestyle and that gave me some trouble as I wanted to get things done quickly. The house we bought was brand new and had no driveway. I called a recommended company. The owner of the company came out in early July and promised to do the job before Labor Day. I said that I wanted it done now. He said, "You better get used to Vermonters. I am one of the few pavers around and, therefore, you don't have much choice. I keep my promises. So, take it or leave it". When I called him in August because he had not even started the job, he almost hung up. He was insulted that I wanted to remind him of his promise.

My wife had found a psychiatrist who seemed to be well-suited to her. My daughter, Lani, and son, John, went to the public schools. It is often very hard for children to make a change. The schools in New Providence were typically suburban type schools with a fairly high pressure environment. Young girls typically paid a lot of attention to clothes and makeup. In the beginning, my children felt that the schools in Bennington were rather backwards. Later on, they both confided that they preferred the schools in Bennington. They felt that the children were less spoiled and more natural in their behavior, and the teachers were more attentive to the needs of the children because, in a small town, they knew more about the families. The school had its challenges as there was a clear division between children from a rural background who really weren't that interested in school, nor were their families, and children who were more likely to be on a college oriented track. When Lani and John went on to the University of Vermont, they both reported that they had been well prepared for university work.

My first week at the college proved to be interesting. Bennington has a gorgeous campus of attractive buildings on 600 acres of rolling hills. The campus includes a former mansion and a barn, which is used as the administrative building. I had six women working in my office. The office manager was a petite woman who was a typical Vermonter. I really had to prove myself to her before she would carry out my instructions. She knew the college inside out and was not afraid to give her opinion on everybody who worked there. She proved to be a delight and was very bright with a no nonsense approach to everything. I didn't take long to bond with all the people that I worked with, which almost made the office feel like an extended family.

During my first week, I had some unusual previews of our students. One day, I noticed a Rolls Royce station wagon parked near my office. I inquired about its owner. I found out that it was owned by a student. I met him, and he told me that his father had promised him a car for his birthday. He told his dad that he didn't want a showy car. His father decided to solve that problem by asking Rolls Royce to make a station wagon so that it would look more functional. A few days later, another student came storming into my office. He was complaining bitterly that the dean of students was a phony. He explained that he had a girlfriend, and he had asked the dean if it was permissible to have the girlfriend live with him in his private dormitory room. The dean had said no. The student felt that a marriage license was a phony thing and that Bennington should be sophisticated enough to let him do his thing. He wanted me to talk to the dean and solve his problem. I was totally unprepared for this. My business career had certainly not trained me for this kind of problem. The boy was quite abusive, and I told him that that sort of behavior was definitely unacceptable. Unless he acted more civilized, I would not discuss it. He left abruptly. A week later he came back. He apologized for his rude behavior and then told me that the problem had been resolved. He had apparently had a big blowout with his girlfriend, and he never wanted to see her again. I took the opportunity to point out to him that that was maybe why the idea of a marriage had been invented. You need to think long and hard before starting a serious relationship.

I worked hard to become familiar with the college operation. There is a basic difference between a college and a business corporation. A business has making money as its prime purpose. The main purpose of the college is to educate its students. This means that there should be an environment conducive to learning, including an uninhibited freedom to exchange ideas, both by faculty and students. This type of freedom almost creates a cumbersome and archaic democracy. Everything is debated and rules are disliked. From a financial viewpoint, there is constant pressure to get more discipline, to go with the commercially viable, which tends to curtail the freedoms that are so necessary. However, the other side of the coin is the responsibility that this freedom carries with it. There has to be some code of behavior and that, in turn, can also become a source of over regulation. Every college has struggled with these issues, and there are no easy solutions. I believe that the best investment, because of its highest return, is to get the best possible people for the various jobs. Colleges have come a long way to even begin to start recognizing this fact. The democratic philosophy that should be the essence of an institution of higher education requires a better support system than is needed in the average corporation. Besides the technical expertise that an employee has to bring to the job, he or she should actively participate in the educational effort. This participation should include both setting a good example with respect to appropriate behavior and also real involvement with the students. While at Bennington, I saw more and more the deterioration that is happening in our society with broken homes and neglect of children. It expresses itself in so many ways when these young people enter college.

I did the usual reviews of administrative functions and found that there were quite a few capable people in the office. The main problem was that, under my predecessor, disagreements had occurred and communication had broken down. In fact, many people had stopped talking to each other. I was able to bring some peace to the operation, and together we started to find ways to improve the various administrative functions. We produced monthly reports. I tried to practice what I had been taught. Accounting should be a form of communication so that the recipients, such as management and the board, could understand what was going on and could, therefore, make informed decisions. Prior to my arrival, the board had to wait until the end of the year to receive the accounting report and, once they had received it, could not understand its contents.

These were interesting challenges. The painful one was that the college really didn't have enough money to operate properly. A number of times I didn't know on Monday how to cover the payroll on the next Friday. Several times, I had to call my friend Dickinson, and he helped me out without any questions asked. He was a true friend. The president had full confidence in me, and we worked very harmoniously. We had to start from scratch and develop a budget that we could afford. I convinced the bank to help us during this transition period as I was confident that, with the proper approach to the alumni and the board, we could raise enough money to make the college viable. The two banks that I dealt with were very supportive and fortunately had enough faith in me that they were willing to loan us money on reasonable terms. We not only had to look at how we could cut costs by eliminating inefficiencies and luxuries, but also had to look at increasing enrollment and getting everybody behind the fund raising effort. In addition, we needed to help the board by giving them current and reliable data and educating them about the college's fundamental problems.

I have found the boards can be a great help or can be a dangerous drain on a college. Many colleges do not think through what kind of people and what kind of expertise they should have on the board. Fortunately, the Bennington board had a group of people, primarily women, who were extremely devoted to the college. They were open to listening to management's views on what had to be done. It was an impressive group of people from the standpoint of financial wealth. It included Fairleigh Dickinson, the daughter of Averell Harriman, a family member of the Johnson Wax Company, and the only daughter of one of the richest families in New York, to mention only a few. I was encouraged by their spirit and willingness to really help. However, although all of them were giving substantially of their time, most were more cautious about making substantial gifts. I have found that most people want to be convinced that they have a winner before a major gift is given. I also found, on my many trips around the country meeting with alumni, that many wealthy women had married men with no wealth. These women often gave large amounts of money to their husband's college, particularly if that would be important for the husband's career. However, it took a long time to convince them that their own college was just as important.

The woman that was the chair of the board was a very bright and "with it" type of person. She quickly grasped the basic issues and also really understood what Bennington was all about. She herself was a graduate of Bennington and had a successful career. She was married to a Canadian oil tycoon, but remained unpretentious. The prime challenge was to get the board interested in fund raising. We had a number of false starts. We hired one expert in the area of fund raising who came to us with the highest accolades. However, during his tenure, I heard various alarming stories from the staff. They were frightened because of his strange behavior. However, he appeared to know his business, so we gave him the benefit of the doubt. Then, one day, I received a letter from him which he signed as Kaiser Wilhelm in which he claimed that he was being pursued by the FBI and the CIA. At this point, I did some further checking and found out that his previous employers had actually been afraid of him. They had withheld the truth about his strange behavior. They knew that he was a very sharp individual who might sue them if they said anything. We were able to get a psychiatrist and family to help us, and he left quietly. We finally hired a professional who was up to the job.

Senior management was also involved in the fund raising effort. Our president got involved reluctantly. He felt that it was humiliating to go to the rich alumnae and ask them for money. I was also involved, particularly in getting our files in order. The college files were totally lacking and, in the beginning, we just had to make the best of it. One day, there was an article in the newspaper about a woman who was the sole heir to an estate of over one billion dollars. Her father had recently died and, upon checking, we found that she was a Bennington graduate. The president and I arranged to meet her through the kindness of a friend who was also a Bennington alumna. When we had lunch at her house, she said that she had no use for Bennington as they had never had the courtesy to answer her letters. She stated that she felt that Bennington had done her a world of good but that, ever since she graduated, they had lost any interest in her. We tried to convince her that things had changed. We told her that there was a real necessity for faculty and alumnae to work together to help the college survive. We hoped that she could help in this effort. Sometime later it was reported, through our mutual friend, that she didn't care for the president, but that I had made a favorable impression. When I was able to do so, I returned to the west coast to meet her again. She was very hospitable, but I had to promise her not to ask for money as she still was upset with the college. I promised that I would not and, instead, talked about the current state of affairs at the college and solicited her ideas. I ended up making three more return visits and, in each case, did not ask or discuss money. Just before Christmas, I received a handwritten letter from her wishing me a Merry Christmas and saying that she wanted to do something for the college. A check was enclosed for two hundred thousand dollars. From that time on, she became a regular supporter of the college. It turns out that fund raising is not as mysterious as people think. At the college level, it has to start with the board's active involvement, including giving meaningful amounts themselves. Then, there has to be a proper match between solicitors and potential donors. Despite the slow start, today Bennington does quite well at raising money for the college.

The college has some interesting faculty, especially in the fine arts.

One music professor with a national reputation was well known for experimenting with new ideas. I went to a concert where the audience sat in the center of the hall. The Bennington choir entered the hall on bicycles. They biked around the audience and sang as a group. Then, at specific moments, soloists would separate from the group and bicycle alone and sing their solos with the choir following behind. It was quite impressive. However, the audience began to get stiff necks as the audience members had to turn constantly to follow the moving choir. In another experiment, he had developed a computer program that, with the clapping of a hand, would direct a rhythm synthesizer to change rhythm. Each time, the rhythm would be more complicated. As this was happening, the professor was playing drums against the synthesizer. This was to be an allegory about man versus machine. In the art department, I didn't care for most of the paintings and sculptures that were created. However, a number of graduates became very famous. A lot of the sculptures were displayed outside on campus making it, in the opinion of many, the equivalent of a sophisticated junk yard.

I had some interesting dealings with the students. One day, I got a letter from a former student who was an Iranian. He had not gone back to his county, but went instead to England. He wrote that he appreciated that the college had advanced money to him so that he could buy a car when he was a student. He had never paid the loan back, but now he was enclosing a check to pay off the debt. I checked our records and could not find anything about such a loan. Apparently, my predecessor had taken it on his own to give him the money. I would never have collected it if the man had not been so honest. Sometimes, we found the opposite to be true. When we tried to collect a substantial amount from one student's parents, they turned out to be professional cheaters who moved from state to state to stay ahead of their creditors. We finally tracked them down in Alaska. However, we found that to legally pursue these people would take years and a lot of money. You may ask, "How could these people get away with running up such a substantial tuition bill?" At the time, it was not customary for a college to have a credit check done. Actually, in general, the bad debts of a college are much lower than in industry as most parents do honor their obligation. However, some parents and students are very ingenious with their excuses. We usually gave them the benefit of the doubt. Now, colleges are much stricter and have better controls. Some students would convince their professors not to report to the administration that they were in class. They would come up with some good story to mislead the faculty member. The business office had no clue that the student was attending. Hence, no collection effort was made. We even caught one student who had loaded dormitory furniture on a truck and was selling it right in the town of Bennington. There were many ways to be creative. One student from Turkey could not get a permit from the Turkish government to have Turkish money converted into dollars to pay the tuition. To solve this problem, his family sent him Persian rugs which he sold to pay his tuition. Then, you had the irresponsible parents. One woman wrote that she could not afford to pay for her daughter and felt that the school should waive tuition. She explained that her former husband refused to pay for his daughter, although he was a wealthy man. Her current husband also refused to pay because he felt that the first husband should pay. Of course, we did not accept this "solution" and eventually got paid. A sadder situation involved a very responsible student who did very well academically. I called her into my office as her parents were seriously behind in paying their bills. Her father was one of the leading lawyers in California and probably had an income of over a million dollars. She said that her father was so busy that, every time she called, he was not available. I told her that this time we should both try to call. I would get him on the phone, and then she could talk to him. I called and got the usual answer. However, when I explained to his secretary that her boss's daughter was going to be expelled from school because of non-payment, the secretary all of a sudden found a way to get him on the phone. I explained to the father how he had embarrassed his daughter and how this embarrassment was even worse as she was one of the top students. The daughter then spoke to her father. Apparently, the guilt feelings got the best of him, and he paid the fees.

Dealing with the union that represented maintenance workers and food service employees was another challenge. Over the years, the college had surrendered a lot of rights and benefits to the union. The result was that, even if I found a man sleeping under a tree, he could not be fired. When the union contract came up for renewal, we exchanged our demands and their demands for negotiation purposes. The union's office in Albany sent a negotiator to deal with me. It soon became clear that the first chapter in that drama was that the union negotiator had to make a good showing for the membership in order to demonstrate that their union dues were well spent. He accused the college of all kinds of things and yelled and showed anger. However, after that useless meeting, he took me aside and whispered that he wanted to talk to me off campus without the union members. We had lunch. He was very forthright. He told me that the membership at Bennington was so small that it was not economically very practical for the Albany staff to spend much time on the negotiation. He asked me for the bottom line and, after some haggling, we agreed on some basic points. At the next meeting, he did a masterful job getting his union brothers and sisters in line. The final outcome was satisfactory to our side. At the next contract negotiation, we had another union negotiator who was more typical, trying to convince me that we were exploiting labor. These negotiations were endless and frustrating, but we were able to come up with a reasonable compromise. Meanwhile, the union members felt more and more shortchanged by their union. Therefore, in the next round of negotiation, I dealt primarily with the actual membership and found it more productive for both sides. The union seemed to have outlived its usefulness. Union negotiators had become used to an adversary role, rather than showing some trust in the school management to work toward a partnership approach. At one negotiation, I recited from the Bible to instill some thoughts of caring and mutual trust. The union was flabbergasted at my doing this and probably thought that I had gone off the deep end.

One very unexpected pleasure during my time at Bennington happened when the board chairperson heard that I was planning a trip to Holland. She invited me to join her and her husband on their private plane as they were going to England at the same time. The plane was a Boeing 707 and was refurbished with a sitting room, a dining room and bedrooms. They had a chef and stewards and a phone to call anywhere in the world. I was even able to do pushups as we were flying at 30,000 feet. We landed at a private airport where customs and limousines came right to the plane. Unfortunately, my hosts were heading to a different destination, so I had to pay for the long trip to

London. The limousine cost me almost half of what the airfare would have cost, but I arrived in style.

Back at Bennington, a new president had arrived on the scene, as our president had assumed the chancellorship of the City University of New York (CUNY), a university with a student population of about 178,000. Surprisingly, he ended up finding CUNY easier to manage than Bennington. Our new president was the number two man at Johns Hopkins University. He was a very dynamic and bright person with a background in philosophy. Unfortunately, the academic training in philosophy does not help much in solving the day to day problems of an institution like Bennington. He tried everything and anything to get the faculty to change their policies and customs. He suffered as much as the former president in this effort.

One of his major efforts to find a financial solution that would bring the college back into a healthy status was a proposed "Lease Back" scheme. The idea was to sell the whole campus to a group of investors who would lease it back to the college and eventually donate the campus back to the college. The investors would have tax advantages which could make the scheme advantageous for them. A well-known law firm had worked out the mechanics, and we had progressed to the point where it could be implemented. In our research, we found that municipalities and even the military had used this technique. We had warships that were owned by private investors and leased back to the navy. The beauty of the scheme was that the navy, for example, didn't have to show the warships as a line item in their budget as it was outside financing that was used to acquire the ships under this method. We had kept this effort under top secrecy to keep the rumor mill quiet and the anxieties to a minimum. When the deal was pretty well complete, the president decided that he should inform the faculty at the next meeting. He asked for their cooperation in keeping it quiet. However, after the meeting, one faculty member promptly informed the local newspaper. The paper wrote a brief article. The Associated Press, which has readers who scan newspapers for interesting stories, picked it up and put it out on the wire services. Pandemonium took over. Universities and colleges called us to see how this was done. The Congress also began to investigate and pushed a bill through that made this kind of deal unattractive. They even went as far as making this new law retroactive to prohibit Bennington from participating in this kind of arrangement. Bennington had not done anything illegal, but had just worked to take advantage of the existing tax laws. For years, people remembered Bennington for this inventive financial proposition.

I kept busy fund raising and, one time; it resulted in a rather amusing experience. We had carefully planned a reception for Fairleigh Dickinson where we would honor him and eventually ask for a major endowment gift. I was to meet him at the local airport in Bennington. The actual meeting went completely off track. I went to meet him at the airport in the late afternoon and then was to take him to a reception with specially invited guests. The private plane arrived an hour late. When I picked him up, he said, "Jim, I left in a great hurry and now I realize that I forgot my toothbrush and my pajamas. He asked if I could take him to town so that he could buy these necessities. I realized that, if we did that, time was running out for the reception. I made an impulsive decision. I said, "Dick, I have to make a confession. We have planned a ceremony honoring you after which we planned to ask you for a serious amount of endowment money. If I take you to town, the whole time schedule will fall apart. So, I propose that, if we do go into town, I will ask you now for a major gift, and then we can skip all the other proceedings." He laughed and said, "I knew you fellows had something up your sleeves. I anticipated a request for a gift. So, I accept your proposition". I told him that this was probably the most expensive toothbrush and pajamas that he would ever buy. I called my superior to tell him of our change of plans and, later on, when the president asked for a gift, Dickinson was ready and made a major commitment.

Another time when I picked up Dickinson at the airport, and as we were driving to the campus, Dickinson said rather hesitantly, "Jim, I have a proposal for you that might be embarrassing for you and for me. I feel that you saved the college and, therefore, I would like to make a donation to the college that will be used to increase your pension and also to benefit another employee who has been instrumental in helping the college". I was embarrassed by the generosity of the offer, but was very honored and delighted to accept it.

At home, things were a mixed blessing. My mentally impaired oldest daughter had been living in a group home and was now being trained to live in her own apartment. Under federal rules, people can only live in a group home for a certain length of time. Nancy was moved to a nice apartment and, in the beginning, it went well, although I had a feeling that it was not going to work in the long run. She had started to regress and, when I moved to Bennington, she went totally out of control. My other children were doing well in school, had made some good friends, and, in general, had assimilated well. My son, John, turned out to have a green thumb and was making extra money taking care of people's lawns. My youngest daughter, Lani, did some babysitting. Sometimes, she was exhausted as she got totally involved with the children and didn't know how to say enough is enough. My other daughter, Joyce, was doing well with her expanding family. She had two children and proved to be a very devoted mother. I disagreed with some of her ideas about how to bring up children, and it took me a long time to stop interfering and keep my mouth shut. My wife, Dorothy, was under regular psychiatric care. She tried to be a good mother, but was really unable to handle that responsibility.

I had made some nice friends through our active participation in our church. I especially liked our minister who proved to be a valuable friend. He was the kind of pastor who never demanded that you should believe in a particular way. However, he was very definite about how a Christian should live and was very active in helping the unfortunate in our world. He created a congregation that was of a similar mindset. It was very inspiring to me. I felt that, at each service, I got a good measure of inner peace.

At Bennington, after the demise of the "Lease Back" scheme, we decided to do the next best thing and went for a bond issue. Given the financial state of the college, it was going to be a challenge, but it was the only way to give the college some reasonable working capital until fund raising would bring in some meaningful money. I had been careful to make sure that the college met its obligations on a consistent basis and had built up a very good relationship with our main bank, the Chittenden Trust. I found that banks in a small town have more trust in the people they deal with because they get to know them better than is possible in a big city. The bank agreed to underwrite the bond issue. Now, we had to get the approval of the state official who was responsible for any public bond issue handled in Vermont. We had to deal with a typical Vermont situation. The bonds were handled by one man who did this work from his home. All the files were at his home and, since he had done it for time immemorial, if his house were to burn down, the state would be in big trouble. There was an official board appointed by the state, but I found out that it still was a one man decision. I went for an interview with the man, and we hit it off quite well. He was a real character–the kind of person that you would like to be friends with. He told me that I should show up for the board hearing. I asked him what I should bring. He said, "Just listen. If there are any questions, I can usually answer them". The board meeting went well. He presented our request and gave his overview. He announced that he favored the public bond and the deal was voted and done. Later, I was involved in a bond issue in Massachusetts and had a completely different experience. Every lawyer and participant had their hands in the process and cost of issuing a bond was almost prohibitive, though very lucrative for the underwriters and the lawyers.

One of my friends at Bennington was a woman who had worked for the college since she graduated from the college. She was one of the earliest students and attended when Bennington was still in its formative stages. She knew practically every alumna and their families. She was a delight and really devoted her life to the college. I found that working in a college environment has a great advantage over the business environment. You deal with many creative people in a setting that is conducive to creative thinking.

I also had time to take on other activities. I was the treasurer of our church and sang in the choir. I became a board member of the United Counseling Services and later became board chairman. I found that to be a very challenging task. United Counseling Services works to strengthen the community through its behavioral and development system of therapeutic, educational, and supportive services for children, adults, families and seniors. The director was trying to make the operation more self sufficient and tried to convince her colleagues that there is nothing wrong with charging clients according to their means. This conversion from a free service to a more business-like operation proved to be very difficult as the professionals really felt humiliated that they had to discuss fees with their clients. The director was a very knowledgeable professional and would not take no for an answer. This created a bad situation, and we finally had to let her go. She had been able to turn the agency around and make it a more efficient operation. I was quite impressed with the improvements. However, in a small town, people hear about every problem. Because of the director's management style, the agency started to get a bad reputation while, in fact, it served the county better than ever.

Being associated with a college like Bennington brought many benefits. There was access to all kinds of plays, concerts and lectures. In the past, I had never had the opportunity to listen to poets or writers. I did so at Bennington, and it was very rewarding. We had some outstanding poets visit the campus. One said that he felt that the clergy watch over men's souls to prepare them for the hereafter, while poets watch over men's souls in the present. I listened to Bernard Malamud talking about his writings. He emphasized that a good writer is one who writes down his thoughts and then rewrites and rewrites and rewrites. And, then there were the beautiful clay tennis courts with a view that was breathtaking. I am a tennis freak, and the courts were in peak shape during my tenure. I also learned cross country skiing the hard way with lots of falling. I found it to be an inexpensive way to get fresh air and lots of exercise.

One pleasurable pastime for me during this time was my piano studies. A Bennington mathematics professor was also an accomplished piano teacher. He also happened to be from the Netherlands. He had taught both mathematics and music for a long time. He had a very talented family who were all involved in music. His wife and his five children had, over the years, built a summer music camp. They had moved into a huge old house and had installed forty pianos. For four weeks in the summer, they had young people from 6 to 21 years of age from all over the world in their camp. The attendees had total emersion in music in a camp setting. Many of these young people were uniquely talented. Every week, they held a concert for the townspeople. It was a privilege to study with the professor who was a marvel, if not a genius. He could yell at me in English and in Dutch when I made a mistake. His teaching was inspirational. He always accentuated the positive. One time, I couldn't get a rhythm right. He said, "I will write it out for you". He wrote above the notes, "Pass the God-damned butter." That did it for me. We became close friends and, for awhile, after I had moved to Plaistow, New Hampshire, I would go back to Bennington one weekend a month to take a lesson with him.

One ritual that I started at the college was to have a contest among all the foreign students to prepare a typical dish from their home country. The winners would receive prizes. It was a great success as the students, both male and female, would knock themselves out to do something special. I entered the contest one year as I believed that I could make a terrific Dutch butter cake. It proved to be very expensive. I couldn't find the recipe. I called a relative in New York and Boston and spent more money on the phone than on the ingredients. Nevertheless, I got the recipe, made the cake and then took myself out of the contest as I felt that my butter cake was so superb that the others wouldn't have a chance to win. However, at contest time, I found out that my butter cake was far overshadowed by some of the masterpieces created by our students.

At home, Dorothy seemed to deteriorate further, and this led to a major turning point. One day, my sister-in law called just as I was returning from work to tell me that my brother had suffered a heart attack. As we were talking on the phone, my wife asked who it was and shortly after said that I should hang up. I kept on talking, and she became very angry and accused me of having an affair with my sister-in-law. That accusation hit me so hard that, right then and there, I realized that she really needed to be cared for in an institution. I talked to her psychiatrist who told me that he was planning to talk to me to suggest that she go to a clinic for further observation. He said that he was willing to sign an order to force her to go if she refused to go voluntarily. Getting her there was one of the most nerve racking experiences for me as I didn't know whether she would stay calm in the car. It was about an hour's ride to the clinic, but it went without a hitch. She stayed there for a month. Although they had access to her twenty-five year medical history from various psychiatrists, they decided that she was able to live at home. They didn't do any follow-up with her, but really just dropped the case.

I started divorce proceedings. We moved Dorothy to a very attractive apartment. Our minister helped us with the move as he also understood that I couldn't continue to live with Dorothy. We watched her closely, and it soon became clear that she couldn't handle it on her own. The kitchen was filthy with rotten food. She acted as if this was a temporary vacation for her and that soon she would return to me. We then got help from a social agency, and they were able to put her into a supervised group home.

Divorce proceedings, under any circumstances, are terrible. The court appointed a guardian for her, and my lawyer and the lawyer for Dorothy started to negotiate. Since Dorothy was totally irresponsible with money, I insisted on a lifelong income agreement rather than a lump sum payment. We finally agreed on a modest lump sum and a guarantee for lifelong income plus a life insurance policy in the case of my death. This has been a very expensive arrangement for me, but I am convinced that it was the right thing to do. At this writing, it is about 25 years later. She now lives in a supervised home for elderly people.

Over the years, I had grown very close to both my brother and my sister-in-law. They both helped me immensely during these difficult times. Thankfully, my children completely understood what I was doing and were very helpful in their own way to get me through this demanding period. Looking back, I often ask myself why I waited so long because my married life was a disaster. I still don't know whether it was out of a sense of duty and loyalty, or pride and an unwillingness to admit to the world that our marriage was a failure, or my concern that a split would be devastating to my children.

I was now living in my house along with my daughter Lani and a student guest from Brazil. One night, I woke up and could hardly breathe. I tried to call my daughter in the next room and somehow was able to wake her up. She and our guest were in total panic. I felt very self conscious about my situation. They called emergency, and I was admitted to the hospital. Meanwhile, my breathing was back to normal with the help of some oxygen. They did the usual tests and were not sure whether or not I really had had a heart attack. They put me in intensive care. Since I now felt much better, I asked the nurse for a phone. She apparently was new and didn't know that a phone in intensive care was strictly taboo. I was now my usual self, always worrying, and wanted to call people to cancel my appointments. In the middle of my phone calls, my doctor came in and, just as he entered, I started to faint. I will never forget his face. It was ash gray as he bent over me and yelled instructions to the nurses. He saved my life. He told me that I was actually dying right before his eyes. I really didn't want visitors as it was a strain. Everybody wants to talk and assure you that you look just fine. The exception was my minister who came in, took my hand, and prayed. He didn't start a conversation, but did everything that he could to make me feel at peace.

The flowers and presents started to flow. One person sent me a very funny little bird with metal legs which you could wind around the bed railing. It put me in a good mood and, later on, the woman who sent it became my wife. Overall, it took me six months to recover. However, now my heart is in better shape than it was before my attack.

Back at the college, the president had decided to take a position at the University of Maryland as the chancellor of the Baltimore campus. The chairman of the board, who was also a lawyer, wanted to act as interim president. He felt that, as caretaker until the college found a permanent replacement, he could do the job by working half days at the college and, the rest of the time, he could maintain his law practice. However, the president of the bank, which was financing the college, insisted that I become the interim president. I was not overly keen to take that position as I was still recovering from my heart attack and know the stresses of the job. The bank manager, the lawyer and I had a meeting, and the lawyer made it very clear that he would fight in any way necessary in order to get the appointment. The bank manager agreed to have the lawyer pursue the candidacy. He met with the faculty and was fiercely attacked for his plan to work half-time while getting, in their opinion, a high salary. I was impressed at how he defended himself. It was like a trial lawyer defending a client. At the end of the session, the faculty almost begged him to take the job. I worked with him and felt that he was quite a reasonable interim. He was a practical man who got things done. He certainly had learned enough about the college as a board member and chairman to handle the political end of the job. I stayed with the college until 1986, at which time a new president was chosen who wanted to bring in her own team. The college gave me a generous severance package, which included a contract with a firm that specialized in finding jobs for executives over fifty-five years of age.

In my seven years at Bennington, I had made some good friends and had helped the college to survive in one of its most difficult periods. I found the quality of life there to be better than in the city. Nevertheless, because of my workload and family difficulties, it had been taxing.

During the last year at Bennington, I became seriously involved with Carol, the woman who had sent me the little bird in the hospital and who also was a member of the church choir. She was a school teacher and well recognized as one of the best in the Bennington school system. Her family had lived for many generations in Vermont. I had done some deep thinking about who I was and what I looked for in another person. I felt that similar interests and a similar approach to life would enhance the outlook for a happy marriage. I felt very comfortable with Carol. A number of years earlier, she had divorced her husband. As a single mother, she had brought up her four children on a school teacher's salary. The children were now grown and were doing well. They had all completed college, including one who initially did not go to college, but later attended and received a teaching degree. I think that a marriage partnership is one of the most difficult undertakings in life. When the initial glamour fades, the essence of mutual trust and support and comfort should grow to make the marriage a real union. Somebody once told me that, in a first marriage, the real test doesn't come until you have children, as children require parents to make sacrifices in many ways. In a second marriage, it is necessary to be flexible with respect to the life that you were used to and be willing to give up some ingrained habits. In our case, with four children each, although grown up, many issues come up that require understanding by both partners. I joke about a stubborn Dutchman marrying a stubborn Vermonter who, on top of that, was a school teacher. Our marriage has proved to be a great blessing. Since I was not used to a full marriage partner, I now realize what a good marriage can be and how much I had missed.

Our wedding was a very enjoyable event. Our minister went through the protocol of discussing various aspects of marriage with us. He was a close friend of both of us and apparently wanted to satisfy himself that we were on the right track. He asked us figuratively, "How did you both get here?" Carol answered, "I came in Jim's car!" We did have a serious and good conversation. We first wanted to have a very small wedding, but he convinced us that we should ask friends and family to come to the church for the ceremony. We should also have some sort of reception. We followed his advice. It was a beautiful day in April when we got married. When people started to flock into the church, I went to the entrance and started to help with the ushering. The minister came and explained that it was not customary for the groom to also be the usher. During the ceremony, my then one and only grandson was very noisy and, since my daughter didn't want to miss the proceedings, we had to speak a little louder to overcome the background noise. At one point in the service, Carol and I had to read something, and, unrehearsed, we both stopped to get our reading glasses out of our pockets. The audience giggled as we did it so formally and exactly at the same time. When the ceremony was over, we went to our car which had been embellished by a string of cans and other decorative items. My brother had bought a new camcorder and was still practicing with it at the wedding. He edited the results, and the footage turned out to be mostly legs and voices. The game was to pair the voices with the legs. It turns out that a lot of our friends and family have nice legs!

Before we went to the church service, I was sitting on the front porch of our house. I had displayed the Dutch flag in honor of my friend the Dutch Consul who was coming from New York for the wedding. The first thing that he noticed was that I had hung the flag upside down. He was very upset about this. I tried to explain that I was distracted by getting ready for the events of the day. The wedding reception was at our house. The food manager of the college had offered his services to put the banquet together, and it was outstanding. We had a lively crowd. At some point, I was asked to play the piano. All the wedding presents had been put on the top of the piano. With the help of some of the guests, we moved the presents to the bedroom and, unfortunately, in the process got the cards all mixed up. Somehow, Carol managed to maneuver through that minefield successfully.

Carol and I honeymooned at a beautiful Vermont inn in Arlington complete with antique furniture and attractive furnishings. After moving our things into the inn, we then went back to the Public House restaurant in Bennington where we had a nice brunch with the family, which included some memorable speeches. It is a Dutch tradition that participants say some appropriate or inappropriate words at such an occasion. I remember that my brother and my Dutch music teacher came through with some memorable observations. I was remembering that, when I was growing up, family occasions usually started with a speech by my uncle. He usually tried to remember the dead and first my mother would start to sniffle and then my aunt and then the whole family would fall in line.

I can truthfully say that, right from the start, our marriage was as if we had known each other for years. The chemistry worked. When Carol moved to my house, Mr. Sweet, the garbage collector, who was used to talking to my housekeeper, now saw Carol and said, "Are you the new lady who works for Mr. Vanderpol?" Since all our eight children were out of the house, we only had to deal with two cats from Carol's side and our cat and my dog, Susan. I hadn't talked to my dog about the changing situation. Susan was the dumbest dog I ever had. She was extremely loyal, but afraid of everything. She wouldn't leave our premises, but would bark loudly if anybody rang the bell or approached our house. She didn't know what to make of the two cats that Carol brought, but tried to ignore them. One was a Siamese and wanted to claim territorial rights right away. Fortunately, Susan was the diplomat and, in no time, had learned how to avoid the Siamese cat. In a second marriage, each partner has to adjust and perhaps change some lifelong habit. However, in our case, that didn't seem to be a difficult task. I was used to giving orders and expected a great deal of obedience from my children. Carol was through and through a teacher and had the self confidence that she usually felt that she was right. Most times she was. The greatest challenge was to have our children accept the new marriage and for us to learn how to interact with our children. Carol had never been involved with a person like Nancy, with her mental and emotional problems. And, on my part, I was not used to the give and take that existed between Carol and her children. She had been much more flexible with her children than I had been. I found this adjustment to our children to be the most challenging task, especially since some of our children were still quite dependent on us both financially and in other ways.

I had thoroughly enjoyed my time in the Bennington community. Besides my involvement in the church and the United Counseling Services, I also got involved in being on the board of the local playhouse. They had an ambitious program and were looking for a better facility. I am glad to see that, after seven or more years of effort, they were able to raise the money to build a modern attractive theater in Bennington. I was also on the board of the local Community Development Corporation which, with the backing of the government, gave development loans to companies. One of our major recipients was CB Sports, which was a major employer in Bennington and was looking to expand. Unfortunately, the seed money we gave the company had no lasting benefit as CB Sports was offered a better deal from New York State and moved, lock, stock and barrel, to New York. I was also on the board of the McCullough House. This was an estate that had been given to the community by the family to be run as a cultural center. The possessions of the past generations remained in the house and included a wide variety of objects from the nineteenth century. We had a curator who, with the help of volunteers and Bennington college students, catalogued the items. There were mementos from the California gold rush to toys, clothes and books. One day, while cleaning out a closet, they found a large collection of Ansel Adams original photographs of the gold rush. This proved to be worth a fortune as all the pictures were in excellent shape.

We also had many music programs from piano recitals to opera to jazz. I once participated in a Dixieland band that had all the old timers hopping. When you drive through a small town, you often get the impression that the inhabitants are rather sleepy folk and certainly not involved in the kind of cultural activities that you can find in a big city. Nothing is further from the truth. The city can often offer more professional quality but, in a small town, that is offset by the joy of a less competitive environment. People participate for the real joy of it.

In contrast, I remember one time when I worked in Pittsburgh; I got a call from a neighbor in Mt. Lebanon who worked for an advertising agency. He was looking for somebody who would participate in a TV ad to promote a local bank. I said, "Why me?" He said that he thought that I was perfect for the job as I had the image of a responsible, honest citizen. I was flattered and accepted. He told me the whole thing would take less than an hour. I showed up at the piano store where I was to act the part of a father of a nine year old boy. We stood in front of the window admiring a baby grand piano. My "son" asked if we could buy the piano. I was to answer that we couldn't, but if I had only saved up money at the bank, we could have afforded it. I was told that they would pay me fifty dollars for the effort. I showed up at nine o'clock. The first problem was that the producer didn't like the store layout. That resulted in a total overhaul, and I mean total. Two hours later, he started to shoot. We had rehearsed the lines. The first cut was excellent according to the producer but, nevertheless, he wanted to change it a little. It took two hours more to get it to his satisfaction. The producer was cursing that he had to use laymen in a hick town like Pittsburgh, whereas in New York, he would have used professionals. However, the worst was yet to come. The TV ad was shown throughout the day for six months, and I became the object of ridicule by all my family, friends, and colleagues.

Upon leaving Bennington College, I made arrangement with David Corbett to help me find a new job. David was a senior partner in a major employment firm and had just decided to strike out on his own to specialize in assisting executives over fifty-five to find rewarding new jobs. He called his firm New Directions. I was his first customer, and he did an unbelievably thorough job for me. He wanted to meet as many family members and new and old friends as he could so that he could interview them and get a profile of who I really was. He even attended my wedding. He then had numerous interviews with me. We started to discuss what kind of talent and expertise I had and what kind of jobs I should pursue. This is really the hardest part of preparing for a job hunt. The analysis showed that I was very people oriented and that I liked traveling and sports. This opened up possible opportunities in finding positions in sports associations, the travel and hotel business, and fields where I had been employed previously. The cruel aspect of job hunting is the lessening of self worth by employers when they tell you in a nice way that they do not need you or that you don't qualify or are over-qualified. This is where David helped me the most. He reminded me of how much I had already accomplished and explained that the system is such that it normally takes six months or more to find a suitable job. It is really not a question of competency, but rather the search for a good match in compatibility, technical know-how and experience. It is unfortunate that so many people have to go through this rather humiliating experience. There should be a better way.

I ended up finding my new job through sheer luck. I was spending part of a week with my stepson and his wife in Haverhill. Because I stilled lived in Vermont, this was necessary, as New Directions was in Boston, and most of my job hunting effort was in the Boston area. I had made up my mind that I wanted to stay in the field of higher education. My stepson's neighbor saw me coming and going and asked his who I was. After he replied, she told him that she worked for Bradford College and that they were looking for a Vice President of Finance and Administration. After that conversation, I gave her my resume. On Saturday morning, I got a call from the president. He asked me some penetrating questions, and we chatted for quite a while with both of us feeling that the chemistry was working. He told me right away that, in principle, I was hired, subject to a further interview with him and with some of the board members. I had my interviews and was impressed with the board members. One of the members, Mrs. O'Neill, was the sister of David Rockefeller and one of the nicest and brightest women I had ever met. When finding a job, it is as important that you get a good feeling about the people who interview you as liking the work and the particular position. I felt that this was right for me, and later this hunch proved to be correct.

We now had to plan our move to the Haverhill area. I dealt with a real estate firm that seemed to really know its business. We sat down and talked about what kind of house I could afford and which kind of house we would like. When I began to look at houses, there was one house that we particularly liked. It had a very large family room with a cathedral ceiling right off the kitchen. The backyard was over two acres of woods with a small stream at its end. When Carol came, I carefully avoided telling her my preference. I hoped that she would select the same house that I liked. When we came to the house that I favored and when she saw the family room, she said, "Wow!" I knew then that we were sold on the same house. We were told that it was a spec house and that the builder had a good reputation. We ended up buying the house in 1986, just at the end of the housing boom. We found that the builder had made several shortcuts, though these would have been hard to detect when we bought the house. We never got any satisfaction from him to make good on the defects. Fortunately, we gradually fixed them and have lived there happily since. We moved in November, 1986, in the snow. At closing, we planted a dogwood tree which has done well. Moving is quite an experience. For months, you have cartons all over the place. As you get older, you accumulate so much that, even when you thin it out, it is overwhelming. One needs a certain kind of courage and determination to throw things away. Carol has a real talent in making a home comfortable. Fortunately, the furniture that she brought from her house and the furniture that I brought from mine could be accommodated well in the different rooms in our new house. I hate to think what will happen if eventually we need to move to a smaller place.

BRADFORD COLLEGE

Any new job is always different from what you have been told or have seen. At Bradford College, I discovered that the college had been in bad shape for three years, both academically and financially. The Trustees had decided to do some real surgery. They hired a new president, Arthur Levine, who was a scholar from the Carnegie Foundation and who had written articles and books about what is wrong with higher education. This man was now my boss. He had no administrative experience prior to coming to Bradford College and had never managed an organization. Nevertheless, the man performed a miracle. He rewrote the curriculum and put some real state of the art practices into place. He was able to convince the majority of the faculty to support his changes. Because of his leadership, Bradford College was a thriving operation that had received widespread recognition. The college now included a program for freshman where each freshman would meet with a faculty member, a senior, and an administrator to talk about his or her impressions and ideas and to get encouragement and guidance. At the end of the freshman year, the student would write a report about the first year experiences and his or her thoughts about the school and really anything else they wanted to cover. It is amazing how one person can create a whole new mood and attitude. The president was a natural when it came to dealing with people and treated everybody, from faculty to housekeepers, with the same respect. He is a man of great intellect and enormous recall, a walking encyclopedia of education. If he didn't like or respect you, he didn't hide that fact. People in that category didn't last very long. I could see that Arthur had made dramatic strides academically, but the administrative departments were still lagging behind. Arthur told me that he trusted me and would support whatever I wanted to do. This was playing to my strengths. It took me about three years to accomplish that task.

Fortunately, the board supported the president whole heartedly in giving time and money and good advice. There was a family spirit that inspired everybody to do the best that they could for the school. One effort was extraordinary. When you have a board member like Abby O'Neill, you have an asset that is tremendous. She volunteered to travel with Arthur to visit selected prominent alumni to solicit major gifts. People were so honored that she would come to meet with them that they felt that they needed to make a good showing by giving a major donation. In this way, they raised five million dollars. Bradford was fortunate because it had existed for more than a hundred years, and originally, it really was a sort of finishing school for society families. It was similar to the Bennington situation as Bradford also had not made a great effort to raise money for an endowment fund. The board also had some very wealthy women who were alumnae. One time, we discussed a renovation of one of the school's landmark dormitories. One of the women on the board was part of the family that owned Hallmark Cards, Inc. She said that she was willing to help. She was a quiet woman who enjoyed being a board member, but was not that involved in the discussions or otherwise active. She said that she would make a gift. She said that, every month, she got an allowance from her trust fund. Since it was almost the end of the month, she would give whatever the balance was in her checkbook. She pulled out a pocket sized checkbook and wrote the check. You can imagine my surprise when she gave me the check which was made out for $230,000.

At about this time, after we had moved into our new home, I started to receive alarming news about my daughter in Bennington. She was spotted by a neighbor walking around in her pajamas. The social worker had been alerted and was doing her best to remedy the situation. However, gradually the news got worse, and the landlord called me to say that he didn't want to evict Nancy, but all the tenants were complaining about her. He and his wife had tried to reason with Nancy, but to no avail. Then I heard that Nancy might have been assaulted as they had found a cigarette burn on her chest. Somebody had reported that a strange looking man had been seen with Nancy in the street. We were able to get Nancy into the hospital. They would keep her for about a week, but then expected me or the social agency to come and get her. It became a desperate situation. The agency had no solution. However, we did find a group home in Watertown, Vermont, which was willing to have Nancy on a trial basis. The woman who ran the home was very committed to her work, and she had confidence that she could handle Nancy. Meanwhile, I talked to my lawyer as I was concerned about what would happen to Nancy if I were to die. She would be a severe burden to my other children. It was also not possible for us to take Nancy for any length of time as she was in a stage of severe depression and rebellion. I had always lived close by and been able to see her frequently. She really didn't like living in an apartment by herself. Her behavioral problems had accumulated and culminated in this life style.

After a month, I got a call from the woman at the group home saying that she could no longer handle Nancy. I went up to Vermont. Nancy had not improved. She didn't want to move from her chair. They had tried to get her to take a shower, but to no avail. When I talked to Nancy, her eyes lit up, but she still would not respond to anything I asked her. I tried persuasion, patience and threats. Nothing worked. The manager told me that the only chance was to get the registered psychiatrist at the hospital to come and declare her so medically ill that the hospital had to admit her. The doctor was in his eighties and known to be helpful in these cases. Five hours later he came. He talked to Nancy and observed her behavior. He said he was not willing to have Nancy admitted to the hospital as they were not set up for Nancy's situation. He suggested that we get her there anyway, because if we could get her there, they had to keep her for a week. I was desperate as there were no alternatives left. The local mental health agency had sent somebody to see if they could help. When I discussed the situation with their representative, he said, "Let's get her to the hospital and sneak her in". He explained that, if the admittance office saw Nancy, they wouldn't let her in as the doctor had not signed the approval form. He knew that the law was that, if we could get her inside the door on the proper ward, they couldn't throw her out. The next problem was to get Nancy in my car and figure out how to sneak her into the hospital. I physically made Nancy get into the car. The group home employees were not allowed to touch her, so I had to do it alone. It was so exhausting that I almost gave up as she was like a piece of lead. I almost passed out with the emotion and the physical demand as doing this stretched my limits. However, we did get her in the car. The agency worker accompanied me to the hospital. He devised a plan to get Nancy inside the hospital. He knew the hospital and went to get a wheelchair. We would force Nancy into the wheelchair and, as I held her down, he would push the chair to the proper location. We were successful in doing this. The floor nurse was an angel and managed to calm down both Nancy and me. We explained the situation and, somehow, she managed to take care of everything.

I have been lucky my whole life that, whenever I reached a crisis stage, there was always a Florence Nightingale for me. They gave Nancy medicine and were able to bring her into a mode of marginal functioning. The hospital had a social worker assigned to Nancy's case. He told me that the pressure would be on in a week to find another place for her. It sounded like the same old story, but with a difference. This man really cared. He said that Nancy would not leave until he had found a solution, and he would do so even if they threatened his dismissal. He kept his word, and he found a seasoned foster family. Meanwhile, I was able to get the State of Vermont appointed as her legal guardian. So, ultimately, they are responsible for Nancy's well being. It is tragic that our society looks the other way in such cases. Today's homeless are mostly made up of the Nancy's of this world when families have given up caring for them. I pray that my family can and will continue to watch over Nancy after I die.

It has been my experience that it takes a year before you feel somewhat at home after you move to another location. It was especially hard for Carol as she had lived for so long in Bennington with good friends and a good job. She tried to get a teaching job in the Plaistow area. However, she always got the same response: Our budget doesn't allow us to hire experienced teachers because the union scales make it too expensive. Carol was recognized as one of the best teachers in the Bennington school system. This makes it even harder to accept the reality of school systems having to short change their students. My boss helped by contacting various superintendents, but to no avail. Arthur offered Carol a job working in alumni research in the development office. Carol didn't really like office work, but did enjoy the actual research part of the job as Bradford has so many illustrious alumni. She also loves to garden. However, the builder had basically abandoned the idea of putting in some reasonable landscaping. The grass was apparently planted by spraying hydro seed. For the most part, this seed washed away as the front yard is on an incline. In addition, he had not properly cleared the soil, so it contained rock, stumps, and building materials. After some negotiation, the builder finally gave me a $300 allowance for the landscaping. That amount did not go very far. However, Carol went to work and, after many years and a good deal of money, we now have a beautiful front and backyard with lots of flowers including a bed of tulips.

We enjoyed having our children within driving range. There was some competition about the race toward grandchildren. My daughter Joyce had three children. However, Carol had to wait until 1992 before she had a grandson. She is now making up for lost time as, fortunately, he lives nearby and she sees him frequently. We did make some very good friends and, although it really took us, more like three years to really feel at home, we now like our situation.

I would like to mention some other private activities. I joined the Rotary in Bennington and enjoyed it. In Bennington, the Rotary had some very unique people as members. The organization there was always good for a laugh. We would sing Happy Birthday for the birthday boys of the month and, over the years; it had become a contest about who could sing the most off key. Our Sergeant of Arms was also masterful in finding reasons to fine members. The money went to charity, so nobody complained. If the Sergeant didn't like the color of your tie, you would get a fine. If there was a nice article about a member in the newspaper, he would get a fine because he declared that the article's flattery was a misstatement. When I joined the club in Haverhill, I found a similar spirit. One member who had the urge to report at each meeting about the ups and downs of the Bruins had prepaid his fines to get the time. I was also invited to join a men's club dating back to the early 19th century. The club has a membership of thirty, usually passing from father to son. Each member takes turns hosting the club and gives a talk on any subject he chooses. Minutes were kept, and a selection of old minutes is read at each meeting. It certainly beats television and good friendships were formed. Unfortunately, a year ago there was a serious dispute about whom we could admit as new members. We split, and I joined a newly formed group which felt the same as I did about the selection process.

It took us six years to find a church in Andover, Massachusetts where we really felt at home. I became the treasurer and a choir member. I still am most comfortable with a congregation where they give you freedom to practice your own beliefs and where there is an emphasis on helping your fellow men and women. I have also enjoyed my membership in the local athletic club where I still try to play my favored game of tennis two or three times a week. One special event is our annual trip to my brother's home in Martha's Vineyard. It is almost like a pilgrimage. Besides the beautiful surroundings and the beaches, we just have a wonderful feeling being together. They have now built a guesthouse so that my brother's children and mine can get together for the 4th of July weekend.

My work proceeded satisfactorily. I revamped the maintenance department by making it an in-house activity. We modernized the computer systems and prepared better financial reports. I enjoyed meeting with the trustee committees as they were very helpful, rather than a hindrance. The college was thriving, and there was a really upbeat feeling about it. We developed a master plan and got quite specific about building a sports facility. Making decisions in a college is difficult as you have to satisfy so many constituencies. If you don't, disaster can strike as was shown in my later experiences with Emerson College. When a decision needs to be made, it is almost like proposing a bill in congress with lots of public hearings, endless debates and an extreme range of opinions. The challenge is to mold and direct toward a reasonable compromise. We were able to accomplish that. Unfortunately, once this phase of the process is completed, money for the project has to be raised and, during that period, conditions might change which will affect the master plan.

During my work at Bennington and Bradford, I had participated in a number of accreditation evaluations. I enjoyed those days of auditing very much. You always learned from the colleagues who were assigned to the task and from the people you deal with at the college

under scrutiny. One of my assignments was Emerson College. I came
up with a number of findings that went beyond the call of duty and got
together with the president after the evaluations to discuss my findings
and make suggestions. He appreciated that and, in my third year at
Bradford, he called me and inquired if I was interested in becoming
the CFO at Emerson. I told him that I liked Bradford and was not
interested at that time. I discussed it with my president. He was fuming
as he felt that it was unethical for another president to go behind his
back to try to steal a key employee. He wrote Dr. Konig a stinging
letter. Konig responded with some diplomatic justification. However,
in the spring of 1986, Arthur Levine announced that he had accepted
a position at Harvard in the fall. Konig now called me again as he
still had not filled the position at Emerson. I had at that point pretty
well accomplished the improvements that we had started and would be
beginning a period of more routine type work. With Arthur leaving,
the excitement and challenge seemed to disappear. Konig increased the
pressure on me and also made a very attractive financial offer. A major
concern was that I didn't like the idea of commuting to Boston. Konig
told me that, since the whole college had plans to move to Lawrence,
he would be willing to let me work from the temporary offices that had
already been set up in Lawrence. I decided to take the offer as my last
full time career challenge. The college needed substantial guidance in
the administrative area and also, because of the contemplated move to
Lawrence, a strong management team was essential. I informed Arthur
of my decision. He had no quarrel with my news, but said that he would
try everything to keep me at Bradford since he felt that, if I left too, the
college would slide backward. This put a guilt trip on me. It was further
complicated when the Bradford trustee, Abby O'Neill, spent a couple
of hours with me trying to convince me to stay–even promising equal
compensation with Emerson which would make me stick out like a
sore thumb in Bradford's salary scale. It was nice to be wanted so much
but, at the same time, difficult as I certainly did not like the idea that
I was shirking my responsibilities. However, I decided that I had done
what I could for the college and that a successor could maintain the
operation without having to be a genius. I also felt that, at Emerson,
this was the last chance in my career to do something meaningful. I
did feel badly to leave Bradford. I had spent some fine and inspiring

years there, and my time with Arthur Levine was a complete joy. We remained good friends and keep in contact.

EMERSON COLLEGE

On January 1st, 1989, I started my new job at Emerson. It turns out that I totally underestimated what I was heading for. Emerson has about 2600 students which made it large enough to have a real full-fledged business department. This meant that I could really concentrate on the overall needs of the college and have time to think. The department had been without leadership for some time. Fortunately, the Associate Vice President was a very able person with a thorough training in accounting and finance. He also had very high ethics and had no fear of speaking his mind. Many organizations lack a person of senior rank who can say no. Usually the organization man does not make decisions, but just acts to please his boss.

The president, who had been at Emerson for ten years, a long time for a college president, had done a solid job in the academic area. He had attracted an impressive faculty with good formal credentials. He had expanded the physical plant, which included the acquisition of a landmark theatre called The Majestic. The college had been the third fastest growing college in Massachusetts for the last ten years. He had changed the college from being a rather non-descript college into being a respectable institution. His methods were extremely dictatorial. He was jokingly referred to as the Kaiser, and he lived up to his name. Most people were afraid of him. Certainly, administrative people would take a vacation only when he was away. He worked hard and expected that from his workers. He didn't leave anything to the imagination. Things were either black or white. He had a lovely family and entertained his staff at his home. He had built a Board of Trustees who had so much confidence in him that the meetings were perfunctory. He answered most of the questions, and we were told not to volunteer any response unless he asked for it. He was impressed with my business career, and I seemed to be the only one from whom he tolerated a dissenting opinion. I had made it clear during our interviews that I was not going to be a yes man. He welcomed that comment as refreshing. Yet, he did not allow others to have a free reign.

I soon came to the conclusion that his dream of moving the whole campus to Lawrence was in serious trouble. As a college president, you are expected to have expertise in a very diverse range of fields. People do not realize that you run a large hotel operation–dormitories and recreation and other services–as well as an academic institution. You have to deal with faculty, who, if they are any good, are very creative and opinionated people. Particularly because of the tenure system, they are not afraid to criticize everything and anything. The clientele is, of course, the student who is at a very vulnerable stage in his or her life. As well as dealing with these very real parts of his job, the president has to look good, raise money and be a good speaker. No wonder turnover is so high. My colleagues seemed to be nice and competent people, though most of them hadn't had much experience outside the college. Konig, in my opinion, had totally underestimated the complexity and risks involved in selling a whole campus of some twenty buildings and building a new campus. The original idea was promising. The buildings in Boston were appraised at around $120,000,000. Building a campus in Lawrence was estimated at $90,000,000 which would leave an instant endowment of $30,000,000. However, the president had no experience in this endeavor and had no seasoned Vice President of Finance to help him. He had hired a number of consultants partly for political reasons and partly out of friendship, but it seemed that none of them had been properly scrutinized as to whether they were up to the task. One major problem was that the buildings in Boston could not be sold with immediate occupancy for the new owner as he would have to wait for a new campus to be built, and that could not be done until the financing was in place.

Another problem was to find a suitable location for the new campus. When making this decision, it is important to work with both faculty and students. A faculty member could easily rouse his students if he didn't like the plan. Students need to be involved from the start so that, as a minimum, they feel that they are treated as junior partners. This all takes time and, when we also include the obstructions created by some of the companies who didn't accept a buy-out under eminent domain by the city of Lawrence, ultimately the deal was impossible. During the three years that it took to have final approval from the land court and other jurisdictions stating that the city and the college had rightful claims to the land, the real estate values had plummeted. My job was to try to find alternative financial solutions. Konig had replaced his main financial real estate consultant with a new one. He and I worked well together, and we were almost able to resolve the financial dilemma. I was inclined to support Konig on the effort as we would really be trading an antiquated plant for a state of the art facility which, in the communication fields, is important to have. However, I felt that relocating to Lawrence was secondary to having a good work place for everybody. I supported the idea to keep a presence in Boston and put in place a good transportation setup so that everybody could have easy access to both the Boston and Lawrence area.

Konig began to receive threats in the middle of the night through anonymous phone calls and insulting mail. The state, which had subsidized Lawrence to make the deal happen, and the Lawrence officials began to get nervous and put pressure on Konig to keep his promises. When a new appraisal indicated that the real estate might be worth $60,000,000, it was clear that the college couldn't afford to pursue the deal any further. The board was still supporting the president, but everybody was showing the signs of stress. The board voted their confidence in the president by approving a new contract with a substantial raise for him.

I had started my job by being responsible for the finance department but, in quick succession, the president added personnel, maintenance and financial aid to my responsibilities. There was some hidden resentment about my expanding role. This was partly due to the sudden way the president handled it. We had weekly meetings of the senior management. At these meetings, Konig would say, "I have given a lot of thought to what I am going to say. I have decided that Jim should take over such and such responsibilities". He would not have discussed it with me previously. He just announced his decision. In my opinion, he had made decisions in the past that resulted in putting people in jobs for which they had neither the experience nor the talent. This seems to happen when a dictatorial type is in charge, because most people are afraid to take the risk to speak up. However, I found that, at least in my case, if you treated Konig with high regard, but with a reasonable amount of frankness and independence, he respected you for that.

In another venture, Konig was approached by some prominent people in Lowell. They were interested in having Emerson take over a defunct law school. They offered to raise a million dollars and also had a building that would be ideal to house the school there. A law school with a good reputation is a money maker as the school only requires teachers and has no research or expensive equipment to run. The defunct law school had a basic library. I made it very clear that Emerson couldn't afford to put money into the venture. Lowell would need to make a financial commitment of one million dollars for us to consider the offer. They confirmed that they understood. Konig, with all his Lawrence problems, still had the energy to take this venture seriously. We had to immediately start to develop brochures and advertise, hire faculty and a president and start accepting applicants, as otherwise we would lose a year and totally lose momentum. We were able to keep our part of the commitment but, unfortunately, the Lowell people could not. They showed us the building in some detail and the architectural plan. Only then did they insist that Emerson commit to a long-term lease. We found out that some of the people involved were realtors who owned property in the area, and they were gambling that, with an Emerson law school present, the whole neighborhood would get a lift, and they would cash in on their real estate. We told them that this was not part of the deal. We had made it clear from the beginning that we could not make any financial commitment. The speculators then made a lot of noise in the newspaper alleging that Konig was to blame for the failure. That certainly didn't help him with the rest of his problems. It was unfortunate that the deal ended this way, because it could have been a viable undertaking if Konig was not so vulnerable and if the Lowell group had been more forthcoming about the arrangements. Emerson would now have to pay off the hired staff and faculty and deal with the applications that had been received.

With all of this, the strain on Konig was showing and, shortly after receiving his new contract, he announced that he was leaving to assume the presidency of Chapman College in California. The board was in shock, especially since he left them with a rather difficult clean-up job. They appointed a former banker as the interim president. This was a surprise to everybody as he had no experience with a school like Emerson. Everybody had expected that John Zacharis, presently the senior vice president, would be the interim president. However, he had disagreed with Konig on moving to Lawrence and, more and more, Konig was treating him respectfully, but as a figurehead. Just before Konig's departure, a serious disagreement arose during one of the senior management meetings. It got so bad that John got up and walked out. John was a very peaceful and quiet type of scholar who actually lacked aggressiveness, but arrived at decisions with deliberation after taking time to study the matter. He was used to years of Konig handling all meetings with total control. Some others had given up really debating controversial issues. The result was that most were hiding behind a screen of silence.

It normally takes a year to find a new president. The process is costly and time consuming because usually all constituencies play a role in the proceedings. The chairman of the board decided to quit as he had been a staunch supporter of Konig. The board decided to ask a former board member, who previously had quit over a disagreement with Konig, to become a member again. They elected a new chairman. None of the present board members wanted to be the chairman knowing of the divisive problems to be resolved. The new chair was Mrs. Irma Mann who owned and presided over a public relations firm. She had no experience in running a board and was not well informed about the current state of affairs of the college. Through extensive interviews with managers, she tried to learn about the college. Board members were very poorly informed and really couldn't give her the information she needed about the school. I spent considerable time with her to give her some insight with respect to finances and the business end of the school. I spoke very frankly with her, which she appreciated. She appointed a trustee committee to advise her as to how we could get out of the Lawrence commitments with the least amount of damage.

Meanwhile, the search for a new president had started. I had been involved in the process both at Bennington and at Bradford. At Bradford, they worked with a retired dean from another school who had a lot of experience in the process of searching for a new president. The new board chair emphasized the importance of thorough communication between the committee and the various constituencies to make sure that a solid consensus could be reached between the various parties with respect to qualities that the college was looking for in a new president. This required time and lots of open and sometimes private discussions. The chair was a diplomatic marvel. She was not afraid to speak up in her attempts to guide the committee toward a productive result.

Nevertheless, communication was lacking. I had offered to participate because of my experience and being familiar with most of the college's strengths and weaknesses. They did not want to involve me for reasons that were never explained to me. It is ironic that Emerson, a communication school, seemed to attract people that thrived on rumor. Many organizations suffer from that disease, but Emerson topped them all. Since the college was weak in its internal communication, it actually fuelled the rumor mill even more.

John Zacharis started to campaign to be elected president. He emphasized the need for the college to heal its wounds and find a practical solution to the Lawrence situation. He was well liked by faculty and administration. I felt that the college was ready for a period of tranquility and introspection to prepare it for the next chapter. John seemed to fill that need and was a known quantity. Many people shared my opinion. I became a staunch supporter for John's election. John was a little suspicious of me as I was hired by Konig and was a relative newcomer. The committee continued to interview candidates and, after a year, came up with an amazing result. They had finally ended up with three finalists, including John, but announced that they felt that none of them were really qualified.

Meanwhile, the interim president was not able to get any support from anyone at the school. At the opening of the school year, there was always a festive faculty meeting. However, this year the faculty boycotted the meeting to protest the appointment of the interim president. The interim had spent a lot of time analyzing the financial condition of the school and tried to show that the college was in a financial crisis situation. It was true that the college had spent millions of dollars on planning for the Lawrence move, including land acquisition, but most of the expenditure was spent on legal and architect fees. I found the presentation rather naïve as it ignored some of the strengths of the college–namely, a good growth history and good potential to continue that and to raise funds from a lot of very successful alumnae. The interim president was Mr. Doomsday, which was not going to help to solve problems, but exacerbate them even more.

The board finally realized that the appointment of McGilraith, the interim president, was a mistake. McGilraith also started to recognize that his authority was only on paper and offered to resign. This was accepted, and John Zacharis was made the interim president. The board agreed that he would not have to forfeit his chances to be considered for the presidency by taking this appointment. John had to take a lot of insults from the board and from the committee. They kept saying he was a great guy, but lacked the right qualities for the task. Meanwhile, I worked closely with the faculty to advocate for John as the right man at that time to lead the college. An institution is like a living person and, at different stages in its life, needs different expertise to meet different needs. The college had endured a long period of division over the Lawrence move and, therefore, the first priority was to bring a reasonable amount of tranquility and stability to the college. John was a known quantity and most of the faculty liked him. He was very knowledgeable about the college and the field of communication. In addition, he was a very decent man with a strong sense of fair play.

Unfortunately, while all this was going on, the newspapers had a heyday. I decided to go to war with the board of trustees. I talked at great length with Mrs. Mann and told her that the board was still so far removed from the players that it would be good if she and the other board members sit down with us to hear our side of the story. She agreed, and we had a meeting with her and some of the search committee members and managers of the administrative departments. The meeting was a mild disaster. The counsel apparently had been instructed to make it clear that the trustees were the bosses and that they could fire all of us if we didn't follow their orders. The chairman of the search committee felt deeply that he knew what the college needed. He presented his ideas very forcefully–none of which included John Zacharis. He told me privately that most of the people at the college should be kicked out and a complete overhaul should take place. I told him that there were a lot of good and capable people at the college. He grinned and said, "Well, Jim, in my book good people don't make it". The whole meeting was similarly threatening and, therefore, the managers refrained from really speaking their minds. The chair tried to be more conciliatory, but to no avail. The meeting demonstrated clearly how deep the college had sunk and how far removed the trustees really were. The Lawrence problems had still not been resolved. The college was accused of trying to renege on its promises. We were threatened with a major lawsuit. The Lawrence planning director was a very aggressive man, and the Lawrence mayor also joined the chorus of threats. However, the total impasse was finally overcome.

Meanwhile, a committee of trustees was formed to address the problems of the Lawrence situation. The committee was chaired by a prominent trustee lawyer who, with his committee, started to dig into the arrangements that had been made with Lawrence. All of this took a lot of time and the pressure kept building. John made a great effort to reconcile the various factions at the school. Since he was still a candidate for president, he was very cautious in dealing with the various prima donnas but, at the very least, he was starting to move in the right direction. One severe criticism from the board was that he had no business experience. Because of this, John proposed a friend of his who was an alumnus and a successful business man for a position on the board. He was eventually selected as the board had quite a few openings since a number of members had resigned. Chris Beck, the new member, was ultimately made chairman of the board.

However, nothing was really being resolved regarding the Lawrence issues. I had a meeting with Irma Mann and proposed that we have a meeting with a small group of experts, who really knew what the history and the arrangements with Lawrence were, to see if we could come up with a course of action. A counsel, who was very familiar with the situation, the financial advisor to the trustee committee, and an outside lawyer, who was expert in these types of issues, were invited to a trustees meeting. I also joined the meeting. Out of that meeting came some concrete ideas about how to tackle the dissolution of the Lawrence project. We negotiated with the goal of keeping the damage to a minimum and minimizing the fallout in the press. We prepared a fact sheet showing that the college would commit suicide if it had to go through with moving its campus to Lawrence. An independent appraiser was hired to evaluate the Boston campus, and he came up with a value of $50,000,000. There was no way to build an acceptable facility in Lawrence, even if we trimmed down our building plans. Eventually, an agreement was reached as Lawrence realized that they were beating a dead horse. We had to resolve these issues as the admissions effort depends a great deal on the perceptions of the prospective candidates. With the uncertainties about where the school was going to be and the fights at the top and the lack of a permanent president, we were in a really threatening situation. The college survived, and I believe it showed the inherent strength that the college had built in its academic programs and the many capable people it had in its administrative operation.

It became clear to me that one of my main efforts should be to bring as much motivation to my troops as I could and to also instill a sense of confidence that the college would overcome the current setbacks. I believe that one of the responsibilities of a senior manager is to sort the trees from the forest and to get an overall sense of what needs to be done. I had gotten very involved with the students. I had the honor of being elected the adviser to the student council each year I was there. I made good friends and got some insights into their needs. This can be very helpful as administrators usually are too far removed from the students. I also initiated a talent show where faculty, students and staff came together to have some fun. It was quite successful with the students and became an annual tradition. Unfortunately, the faculty didn't like the idea and didn't give it much support. They missed the point that this was an effort to bring the various factions together in a friendly social atmosphere. At Christmas, I organized a little choir to go to the different departments and brighten up their day. It is always amazing how little things like that create so much good will.

Prior to the final dissolution agreement with Lawrence, we had been working with the First Boston Company to refinance the college's outstanding debt. The college had an arrangement with Bay Bank which guaranteed the debt for an annual fee. However, in 1989, banks started to get into trouble and the bondholders of the college were not satisfied with the bank guarantee. The college was now penalized as it had to pay higher finance costs. It also ran the risk that, if Bay Bank really got into serious trouble, the loan might be called, which would create a financial disaster situation for the college. In addition, the guarantee was only valid through 1990, at which time we were totally dependent on the good graces of Bay Bank to renew the guarantee. We knew that it was going to be very hard to find another guarantor because the only collateral that the college had was its real estate. There was no liquid endowment fund. Banks abhor being put in a position where they are forced to foreclose on an educational institution because of the terrible public relations implications. Therefore, I urged the board to work with the First Boston Company to refinance the debt into a long-term fixed rate bond. The current debt had a variable rate which, for a college in Emerson's situation, was in my opinion irresponsible.

It was a difficult time to refinance as the markets were jittery, and Emerson had a sustained bad press because of the Lawrence drama and the turnover at the top. Fortunately, universities and colleges in general have a good reputation in the bond market. I tried to emphasize with First Boston Company that we could show a good growth record and that we had a good finance department which managed to keep budgets in line even with all the turmoil. The bank helped us prepare our presentation to potential investors like Fidelity and other major investors in the bond market. We were fortunate as First Boston Company made two key people available who were really professional and blessed with great brainpower so that Emerson could present itself in the best possible way.

I will never forget the day that we had to make our presentation. Our president, John Zacharis, called me into his office to tell me that he had just found out that he had leukemia and had to leave immediately for the hospital. Of course, he was going to be the prime presenter to sell the investors on Emerson. From previous experience, I knew that the investors would very much look for clues as to whether or not Emerson had good management. Without their feeling of comfort in this area, it was not going to work, especially with all the negatives that Emerson had had recently. It was also true that we practically had our backs against the wall as it would be very difficult and costly to find alternative solutions. Zacharis told me to take charge. I felt confident that, together with my senior associate, we could produce a convincing story. Fortunately we did, and Fidelity announced that they were interested in underwriting most of the $6,000,000 bond. At that point, our new chairman of the board entered the negotiations to help get the best possible terms. Mr. Beck is a good negotiator. He is a very imposing man, both in his appearance and because of his sharp mind. He also does not take no for an answer. He was able to get some more flexibility in the collateral arrangements. All in all, it was a milestone in the college's history as we now had a long-term, fixed rate debt structure and had avoided a serious financial crisis—a sigh a relief for me. Of course, we had to live up to a financial discipline dictated by the tenets of the agreement, but that was actually healthy. At budget time, we had to reduce some of the costs, which we were able to do.

One of the most difficult problems for most managers is to fire somebody or even to let someone go with more amicable arrangements. One of the most difficult tasks I had to deal with was a personnel problem. We had a director of computer services who had been in that job for many years. Budgets for his department were large, but grossly insufficient for meeting the expectations of the users. He had built a very sophisticated set of systems with a strong dose of know-how. He had a senior programmer who was a genius and fanatic about his work. In comparison to what I had seen at the two other colleges I had worked for, Emerson was far ahead of institutions of its size. The trouble was that the programmer was the prima donna type, and the director was not very flexible or diplomatic in his ways. Over the years, this had caused friction and downright animosity, especially with the Academic Dean. She was interested in computers and had learned how to use a PC and felt that she was knowledgeable enough to make that judgment. I disagreed with her critique as the issue appeared to be clearly a personality problem. One time when a problem arose, she told me first calmly and then in a threatening way that I had to fire the director. I told her that I thought that it was a mistake as he was competent, and I was working very hard with him to become more flexible and diplomatic in his dealings. I certainly had tried to monitor him closely and help him and had achieved some good results. Also, since the man had been there for so long and nobody had ever gone as far as telling him that his job was at risk, it seemed that the college would be at risk with a costly suit if it, all of a sudden, took this drastic action. All this was to no avail. The Dean said that either he goes or she would leave. The president at the time, John Zacharis, had several meetings with us. The Dean was unshakeable in her convictions. We then had an outside consultant review the situation, and they pretty well confirmed what I had said. However, the issue wouldn't go away and finally the president told me that, for the sake of peace at the college, I had to let him go. I was extremely unhappy, but I sat down with the man to see what I could do to help him. We negotiated a satisfactory settlement, and I tried to help him find another job. This all happened just at the time that the economy fell apart, especially in the computer industry. I have thought about this many times. Should I have shown more character by refusing to fire him? It ended up that he found a job at another college, and his assistant at Emerson followed him.

It took me three years to finally get the board to accept an endowment policy that corresponded with policies adopted by most colleges years before. The situation was analogous to the Frenchman who put his savings in cash and hid it somewhere. We had cash and money market funds, but no equity securities or other type of investments. The endowment was so small in relation to the operating budget that it could not save the college in any time of financial difficulty. It would certainly not impress any investor who wanted to know whether the college had real collateral security. However, it took me practically my whole tenure at Emerson to get the approval to implement a better endowment policy.

It was suggested by a board member that a college should be efficient, but it is not there to make a profit. There are many overlapping and interdependent departments in a college. The humanities may get fewer students than other departments. The communication fields, which are usually big cost operations because of the equipment and space needs, tended to get the most students. However, humanities are required and have lower costs. In the profit center concept, you would eliminate the communication studies and keep the humanities and, thereby, kill the school. I tried to get this point across, but to no avail.

When I was made the chair of the administrative planning committee, things deteriorated further. Two trustees were looking for a good real estate deal for the college. Meanwhile, my group was looking at the future needs incorporating the academic and finance areas. Our task didn't go very far since there were no clearly stated goals from the board or from the administration because of the turnover in presidents. Because Mr. Beck pressured everyone to move forward, we reduced the task to the immediate needs of the college. The college owned a number of old buildings, none of which were built for the needs of the college. Because of years of neglect, these buildings had been reduced to marginally functional buildings. The cost of the planning for our proposed move to Lawrence had made it even harder to afford adequate building.

When John Zacharis became the interim president, I had discussions with him about the international aspects of higher education. I felt that, especially in the fields of communication, the international aspects became even more important. News broadcasting covers the world. The USA was no longer a dominant monopoly, and more and more American companies had to work with foreign companies and/or compete in foreign markets. The old cliché, the world is shrinking, is correct. Emerson students often would go abroad for a semester. Usually, they would be in a group and live together and often have limited exposure to the foreign culture or daily contact with the local citizens. They would go to museums and theatres, but the experience didn't really allow them to get a real insight into another country or its culture. For example, Emerson had a castle in the southern part of the Netherlands where limited studies were offered. The students would live in the castle, which was very romantic. In addition, the head of the operation did a marvelous job of exposing the students to the local citizenry as much as possible. However, the castle was isolated, the courses very limited and the students were all Americans. My idea was to create a school which would concentrate on the international issues of the world. It would have students from many countries and a mix of professors from different countries. I wanted to use my international business experience as a consultant for Coopers & Lybrand to help Americans establish companies abroad.

If these ideas were to be successful, the venture would help the admission office in its recruiting as more and more parents and students began to understand the need to learn more about the world and be less provincial. Of course, a new venture is high risk and costs money. I proposed to do it in such a way that we would minimize long-term obligations and try to get the local governments involved. John became more and more enthusiastic about the idea. Then a lucky break happened. I was invited to an opening of a new home for orphans in Boston. The funds had come from a prominent Dutch foundation which built these facilities all over the world. The president of the foundation was the governor of the province of Limburg in the Netherlands. He was to officiate at the opening. I didn't know the man. I wrote to him saying that I couldn't attend the opening, but that I would be delighted to meet him for lunch. To my surprise, he accepted the invitation. At this meeting, I told him about my ideas for a European school, and I emphasized that we would insist on quality, a subject foremost in the minds of Europeans. This would be a joint effort and a sound operation. He was more than enthusiastic and asked how he could help. I told him that we needed money, formal recognition, the support of a local university and the right location.

At that time, I had made some contact with the mayor of Amsterdam, who my brother had befriended and who was interested in locating a school in his city. I was comfortable with the idea of settling somewhere in the Netherlands. The Dutch are historically known for their tolerance and are especially friendly toward Americans. The Dutch and the USA have the longest lasting friendship treaty between two nations. Also, almost all Dutch citizens speak English, which would be the language spoken at the school. We had some other contacts in Amsterdam which we pursued. In about three months, we heard from the governor in Maastricht, Limburg. He wanted us to come to Maastricht to discuss an action plan. Meanwhile, Dr. Larry Conner, who was the Dean of External Academic Affairs at Emerson, was officially in charge of developing the school. Since I already had duties as the Financial Vice President of Emerson, I would work more as a consultant. When we traveled to Maastricht, we found that the governor had performed a major miracle. He had passed a resolution in the provincial assembly recognizing Emerson College in Maastricht. In addition, he had obtained an approval for a $450,000 subsidy. He formed a committee consisting of himself, the mayor of Maastricht, the president of the University of Limburg, the president of the Technical University and the Provincial Minister of Education.

Limburg University offered to have their Department of Economics do an independent feasibility study. Both schools offered their library and other services for our use. In comparison, a parallel effort in Amsterdam became a typical bureaucratic nightmare. We decided to go with the Maastricht proposal. Their study was very affirmative. Our own research came to the same conclusion.

We found a unique building right near the Maastricht universities. Our librarian reported that she had worked out a good understanding with the university library. European universities have, in general, been a government operation with age old customs and bureaucratic views. Public and private universities in the United States tend to have much more flexibility. In addition, the idea of preparing students for a career is not customary in Europe. In Europe, universities deal with theories and vocational institutions deal with the "hands on" practical matters. Larry Conner was working with the Emerson faculty to develop a curriculum and to get the faculty involved and supportive of the effort. However, many people feel uncomfortable with anything new. One of my piano teachers compared it to the pushing that one has to do to get a bicycle up to the speed that you need so that you can change gears. Our faculty, like any faculty, had to debate and debate and debate. The faculty finally signed off in the spring of 1991. We wanted to have the first class start in the fall of 1991. This gave us precious little time to recruit students. We also wanted to have the school accredited by the New England Accreditation Association. We met with the president of that organization, and he was so impressed that he said that, if he were looking for a job, he would have liked to become the head of the school. Dr. Conner was able to recruit an Emerson Senior Professor of Journalism as the first director of the school. He proved to be an excellent choice. We also hired an excellent admissions director. She was Dutch and had graduated from Emerson. This was a new position for Europe, because you ordinarily don't need to have admissions personnel because the state universities do not have to attract students.

Tuition rates needed to be set. We decided that US students would have to pay the full freight as they were eligible for financial aid on a need basis. However, Europeans or other nationalities could not get financial aid as the school was not formally recognized by the Dutch or Common Market governments. The Common Market had a substantial fund available called the Erasmus Fund to help education. However, those funds could only be released to schools recognized by member governments of the Common Market. We decided to give the foreign students a 20% discount for tuition, room and board. In Europe, the taxpayer pays for education for everybody up through college. It is, therefore, difficult for Europeans to fork up substantial money for a private school. The public doesn't realize that a university education in Europe costs about the same per student as we pay in the states. However, since it comes from tax revenue, everybody tells you that it is free in Europe. Europeans do not realize how expensive education really is because the costs are hidden in the general tax revenues. Education is not a private initiative. The approach taken in Holland, as to who will be admitted to higher education, is a bit unusual. The government sets the budget and, based on that, figures out how many students can be admitted to the universities. If there is a shortage of funds, they have an annual lottery and those students who win get to attend university, and the rest have to wait till the next year. Fortunately, the government usually has enough funds to keep lotteries to a minimum. However, in general, fewer students attend university than in the US.

At Emerson, as at all privately financed colleges, we had to deal with the complicated aspects of financial aid. Is this to be treated as an expense to the school and show as such in the financial reports, or is it really a discount on the fees charged and shown accordingly? It is a cost to the school but, as financial aid became an ever larger number, it became more important to show its relevance to the tuition income, rather than an expense. Bennington College provides another good example. It is often known as one of the most expensive schools in the country. However, what most people do not know is that Bennington is very liberal in giving financial aid. Some students do not have to pay any tuition at all.

At Emerson, financial aid had been carried as an expense, and no research had been done as to how competitive the school was. I determined that the school was not competitive at all and that there had not been a good analysis of what we should do. Fortunately, I was able to hire a new slate of people to do that job. A person from Tufts, who had a great deal of experience in this area, was hired to put in the many hours necessary to totally revamp the process. We gradually brought the aid programs in line with other schools and started to market our programs. We started to educate candidates that our programs were based on charging students on the basis of what they could afford. With the help of government aid and school aid, very few students would be unable to come to Emerson for financial reasons. Private schools have made a dramatic change in this area.

Our first European class in the fall of 1991 consisted of around 35 students from 17 different countries. They lived in a nearby dormitory and seemed to get along very well. Later on, I heard that some kind of constructive academic rivalry existed. Apparently, the American students found out that the European students were more advanced in certain fields, and they felt challenged to catch up with their European friends. Our professors reported that they found the students in the Maastricht school more challenging than the ones in Boston. The director of the school had done a marvelous job in overcoming the growing pains of any new organization. We had found attractive, good quality furniture and equipment. The building had ample room to make space available for each function. We even made arrangements for a mini cafeteria. A good, all-purpose maintenance man was hired. We set up a computer facility and, later on, expanded it. We had an excellent television studio/laboratory. It is amazing the detail that goes into building a college. The second year, we increased the enrollment to around 60 students and, in 1993, we had 125 enrolled.

One of the Boston professors had organized a special preparatory course so more senior students could participate in the radio and television coverage of the "Maastricht Summit of the Prime Ministers of the Common Market". Unexpectedly, they also got involved in covering the return of Henry Anderson, the journalist who had been held captive by Muslim fanatics. The students had learned about the issues of the Common Market and had had courses in the whole range of subjects dealing with television news casting. In order to get accepted by the pros in the field, they had stretched the truth a little and had claimed to be an association of New England journalists. This way they didn't have to declare that they were students and, therefore, would have a better chance to be taken seriously. The students had specific assignments in preparing background materials, which also made them more knowledgeable about these subjects than some of the professionals. Arrangements had been made to have some of their stories broadcast in Europe and in the states. They were able to get interviews with the prime ministers. I saw the results on video, and it was remarkable. Of course, the students were extremely appreciative that the school had given them this chance to learn.

Another notable effort was the creation of a newspaper. Our director had challenged the first-year students to decide whether they wanted to start a typical student newspaper or create a newspaper for the many foreigners living in the immediate area who really had no newspaper that they could read because of the language. Most of the foreigners used English as their common language. The students started to develop a local newspaper in English, and it was an instant success. I read the paper, and it was refreshing, covering everything from the different prices of beer in the local bars to scientific coverage of environmental topics to local issues. Later on, the college created a local television station.

In the early stages of development, when we wanted to formally announce the opening of the school, the mayor of Maastricht hosted a reception for dignitaries and the press. John Zacharis and Larry Conner were present as well as Manny Paraschos, the newly appointed director, and me. During the press conference, one journalist asked if he could ask a question about the relationship with the president of Limburg University. He stated that his English was not good enough to properly ask a controversial question. I interrupted to remind him that I spoke Dutch just to make sure that he would not use the language issue to get around my American colleagues. His question was, "Why was the university willing to help a potential competitor?" The president answered by saying that the university had decided that the American approach of a practical liberal arts education was a better way to educate students. Therefore, the university had to learn what it was all about. By helping us, they helped themselves and, eventually, the advantages were for the students. The university was serious about this. They have already implemented various changes as a result of this experiment. Since Emerson uniquely specializes in communication, and the university had not much to offer in this subject matter, it would not become a problem.

When you compare the European Common Market with the

American financial markets, you find some basic differences. The United States has had to deal with a mass market for a long time. The Europeans are still divided by country, each having their own type of market and distribution system. The US also had developed advertising techniques to reach large numbers of people who might also be divided into various cultural and ethnic groups. The US also had many more very large multinational corporations, while Europeans had few of that size and type. Further Common Market development would almost dictate that people and companies learn about the US experiences in these areas to avoid the problems that we had faced. It was even more critical that institutions of higher learning should join together to help. However, in my dealings with various companies and individuals, I was always impressed with how many people didn't really want to face issues of change and prefer the status quo. This is true the world over.

We recognized that it would be very helpful to get recognition from the Dutch national government and show that Emerson provided a good quality education. If you use public relation firms to do this, the cost can be prohibitive. Since we did not have funds for this purpose, we started to develop our own plans. To get recognition from the Dutch government in The Hague was especially important because they could then give scholarships to Dutch students. I looked for a prominent Dutchman who could help us. The former governor of Limburg had now started a new job as head of Rodamco, a very large investment house. He didn't want to be actively involved in supporting the school as he felt that the new governor might take exception to that. However, through my Dutch sister-in-law, I was able to contact Paul Schwarz. He was a wealthy and very successful businessman who had just retired from his various ventures and had time to get interested in something new. When I explained what we were doing, he got very enthusiastic and promised to help. What I was looking for was to get a council of prominent Europeans to help guide the school and also to have their names on our stationary, which would be the best name recognition we could get. He was willing to get involved in recruiting these leaders in their fields. I also had talked to one of our Emerson trustees, Vin De Bona, who had made his name producing a series of shows featuring the funniest US family videos. He told me that he had expanded into the European markets and knew many prominent people in the television industry. He was the kind of person who would need little follow-up to get things done. He contacted various television companies in various countries to get us introductions to senior management. Paul Schwarz and I visited these people. We had decided to organize a second council, which would be more technical in nature to advise the school on ways to develop various curricula. These contacts could make this really happen.

The other priority was to have a committee of Emerson trustees get involved in helping to oversee and cooperate on a board level to promote the proper development of the European school which was now called the EIIC, the European Institute of International Communication. This effort got nowhere. Some individuals, like Vin De Bona, were willing to help and took the initiative. Another trustee went, on his own initiative to Maastricht, to evaluate the school for himself and gave a glowing report on what we had done. Meanwhile, I had to suffer from Mr. Beck's jokes at board meetings where he intimated that I participated in developing the European school just to justify free trips to Holland. Larry Conner had been asked to prepare a documentary about the school to give the board a chance to learn more about the school. At the presentation, he was cut short after about five minutes, as they said they didn't have the time available for that subject. It was never revisited at subsequent meetings. Nevertheless, EIIC managed to do well in spite of the lack of support by the board and the turmoil at the top at Emerson.

Paul Schwarz and I were hard at work following up on the contacts we had. Our visit to the television producers had been successful and educational. We talked to one of the main producers in Holland who explained the cumbersome and unworkable system the Dutch government had set up to allocate television time slots. It was based on surveys of viewer interest. The producers had to make a guess regarding when and how much time they would get from year to year. What was also disturbing was the tunnel vision that this producer had about the future of Dutch television. He felt that, regardless of the Common Market, television would basically concentrate on the local country and not really expand into other Common Market countries. I was disappointed, as the Dutch are known to be entrepreneurial by nature. He gave the impression that they had been beaten down by the bureaucracy.

It was refreshing to listen to our contact in Paris. The Parisians strongly believed in international expansion. They had just done something new. They had produced a quiz show for the French audience. Then, they had hired a well-known anchor man to provide a sound track in German, thereby having the cost of one show for two different markets. We then visited the German company and were warmly received. They had bought the video records of all the German news casting since World War II and were interested in making documentaries. All the producers we talked to were interested in getting involved with EIIC. They all complained that the European schools didn't prepare the students for a career in producing and broadcasting shows and that, therefore, they had to do all the training.

Another challenge was to find well-known prominent people who would be interested in spending time and money to help the EIIC and, through their participation, provide name recognition for the school. I visited Ex-Governor Kramer in Rotterdam, and he was most gracious, giving me ample time to discuss potential candidates. We also discussed ways to approach the Dutch government to get official recognition for the EIIC. If we could get official recognition, this would open the door for student scholarships and access to the Erasmus Fund of the Common Market. He also contacted Mr. Deetman, who was the president of what we would call the House of Representatives. He was also the former Minister of Education and the head of the leading political party in the Netherlands. Arrangements were made for Paul and me to meet Mr. Deetman. We had a number of meetings with Deetman and Kramer, and they suggested a number of people who were prominent in government circles and in industry in Holland, France and Germany. Many of these were well-known cabinet members in government and/or in the Common Market. They also followed up and contacted these people.

We even managed to reach the senior level of the Dutch Department of Education. They were not optimistic that we could get official recognition. They were working with shrinking budgets, and recognition would mean that the EIIC would be included in the financial support system. We continued to push the idea that it would give Dutch students a new alternative. They could choose to go to the EIIC instead of the university. It would not add to the budget.

During this time, I also had to handle my duties as Vice President of Finance back at Emerson. However, my dealings with the board of trustees were very limited. Konig hadn't wanted to have his managers participate in trustee debates as he felt he was the mouthpiece for the administration, and he wanted to control what was going to be discussed. This policy continued, to a great degree, under John Zacharis as he also felt that he was responsible for any administration statements, and he wanted to control that. I had good rapport with some of the trustees. When John became interim president, I suggested that he consider a careful selection for any new trustees in order to bring the board in line with current needs. I felt that Emerson had become a national college and, therefore, should have some trustees with national prominence. I recommended two people, one of whom was nationally prominent and the other was an extremely successful fundraiser and was well-known in the entertainment industry. I was putting my personal friendship on the line, but both were interested to join. My second candidate became a member of the board, but resigned later as he was not happy with the board. The other candidate was so poorly handled by Emerson that he never became involved. One of the trustees, Mrs. Rose, was a graduate of the college and had a lifelong interest in helping the college. She had given both time and money. She organized an effort with her socialite friends to form a group called Friends of the Majestic Theatre. Through that organization, she hoped to interest local citizens in supporting the restoration and operation of the theatre. She asked if I could assume the presidency, and I did. It was an effort that was not initially geared to raise major money, but more to get the interest of a large number of people and then eventually work from there to providing financial support. We arranged for parties at the homes of Mrs. Rose's friends. Emerson did a very fine job in providing entertainment by its students and faculty. Mrs. Rose was providing the enthusiasm and the expertise to get the effort underway. There were very few trustees who took that kind of initiative to make things happen.

I was also a member of the negotiating team, which was to come up with a new three-year contract with the faculty. The team consisted of the head of Human Resources, Larry Conner, and me. The academic dean was indirectly involved with the president to set the conditions. I knew that the main task was to overcome the amount of distrust that existed between the faculty and the administration. Most colleges suffer from this distrust, and it is a very difficult problem to deal with. Right from the start, I advocated an educational open discussion about finances with faculty representatives. I emphasized that any legitimate question would be answered and that I wanted to take advantage of the negotiations to really familiarize them with the business aspects of the college. The discussion was well received, and we made a good start in eliminating the many misunderstandings that had been created over the years. Though Emerson specializes in communication, it had done a poor job in its own operation. I had experience negotiating a contract at Bennington with the food and maintenance union. The difference this time was that the faculty was articulate and wanted to negotiate in an educated way; that means, more time for every subject and the necessity to refine the language to such a degree that it either becomes very clear or totally incomprehensible. It took us about nine months of negotiating. We were able to overcome some serious hurdles and outrageous demands and were able to reach an equitable compromise.

The negotiations were concluded in the nick of time. John Zacharis and Jackie Liebergott, the Academic Dean, had given valuable input that helped to bring the contract more in line with current conditions and needs of the college. We, therefore, started the school year in the fall of 1991 with one less source of insecurity. Unfortunately, John had a setback with his fight against leukemia and had to become a part-time president. Jackie Liebergott became the substitute president. In February, 1992, John died, and Jackie was made the acting president. She declared her candidacy for the presidency, but there were some doubts about her eligibility. I had hoped to work two more years before my retirement, and especially wanted to bring the EIIC along to a stage where it was firmly established. My departments were humming along. The finance department had absorbed a steady increase in work because of the expansion of the college, the ever-increasing governmental requirements and the demands of the various groups to get more and better information. We had built a genuine camaraderie in all of my departments, and that certainly helped me to offset the blows I had to take elsewhere. I was really pressuring president Liebergot to sit down with me to discuss issues. She finally agreed to see me on a Monday morning in September, 1992. When I sat down, she handed me a letter stating that I had been relieved of my responsibilities in the maintenance department as some of the residential rooms were not properly cleaned before the students returned from their summer vacation. She also noted a few other concerns, and it was clear that she was not satisfied with my performance.

When we met again, I told her that the demands on me during my years at Emerson had been continuously difficult and that, for health reasons and not to damage the college, I would be willing to resign if we could agree on a settlement. She was relieved, and we started to negotiate with the help of the college counsel who claimed to be in shock about what they were doing to me and the college by pushing me out. We finally agreed on a settlement.

By this time it was summer, 1993. I realized that I just had not been able to absorb too well what I had just gone through. I thought that I was prepared for retirement as I had plenty of interests and had hoped to save enough to be able to do a lot of traveling for pleasure. However, I was used to being appreciated by my peers and receiving formal recognition for a job well done. That was important to me. Now, I had to adjust to a new environment where my wife and friends were the only ones who could let me know that I was all right as a human being. I also had to ask myself whether aging puts you on the wrong side of the balance sheet if you do not produce anything useful for society.

RETIREMENT

When I retired from Emerson College, I didn't have the faintest idea of how to handle retirement. My first idea was to build a pond in the back yard. Carol had developed beautiful gardens as we had a big yard to cultivate. My first try at building a pond was to make a small cement pond big enough for the grandchildren to splash in. Initially it leaked, but putting a rubber liner in it worked. With that venture as experience, I then decided to build a larger pond and fill it with Japanese koi fish. The new pond was initially too small for the fish, and I eventually expanded it to twice the size. To add more interest, I built a sluice by creating an incline with a small reservoir at the top which filled through a hose, using a pump to create water flow from the reservoir to the fishpond. Carol then surrounded the pond with flowers and plants.

I soon found out that I had to buy an expensive UV light to connect to the hose. It was necessary to clean the water in the pond because rainwater and nature's droppings dirty the water in a hurry. I was told, by my pond expert, that I had to clean the pond at least once a year. But, what could I do with the fish when I was doing the cleaning? This predicament led me to build another pond that could temporarily house the fish. I also put extra pumps in the ponds to create fountains to circulate the water. All this required an expanded electrical supply to run the pumps and lights that were added to make the area look romantic at night. For years, it was a nightmare. Many times when it rained, the pumps and lights went out, and it took a professional electrician to solve that problem. However, all in all, I really enjoyed the challenges of the project and learning more about building ponds and fish and the mystery of electricity.

However, when some time later I had the urge to build yet another pond, I knew that Carol would say, "No more!" I needed to come up with a creative idea. Our grandchildren were now older, so my proposal was to build a pond for them with a little beach and a small boat house. Carol was open to this. However, when I needed to get her consent to remove one tree where I wanted to build pond number four, she said, "No way!" I now had to build a pond around the tree and had to improvise to get the rubber liner around the little island with the tree. Since I now had an island, logically I had to build a Dutch drawbridge to get to the island. My neighbor, a retired master carpenter, promised in a weak moment to help me. We built an authentic replica of a typical Dutch drawbridge. My neighbor was professional and a perfectionist. I am impatient and always looking for shortcuts. We made quite a pair. When I had finished the pond, bridge, beach and boathouse, we invited the grandchildren to help with the official opening. Soon thereafter, I found that the rubber lining was leaking as I had to cut it to fit around the island. It was then that my wife suggested that we cut down the tree.

The Fashion Institute of New York

Shortly after my pond building experiment, I received a call from an acquaintance who was now the new president of the Fashion Institute of New York. The institution was part of the New York State University system. He planned to overhaul the whole administrative system and wanted my help. I liked the challenge and spent a year on the assignment. It was quite an undertaking to commute every week to New York by train. During this commute, an engine took off without the engineer being aware of it. Another time, the conductor locked himself out of a railroad car. The air conditioner sometimes broke down. And once, when the engineer couldn't stop the train in time, a man committed suicide by walking on the railroad track. The job itself was almost impossible. The school had an international, excellent reputation. However, the faculty had, over the years, eroded the authority of the president. Labor was highly unionized and added excessive rules. After my audit and evaluation, we developed an action plan. The greatest challenge was how to convince everybody involved that it was to their benefit to reorganize the school, in particular, because of its very serious financial problems. Nevertheless, many were intransigent, and it was truly a nightmare. Results were mixed and, some time later, the president resigned.

The United Way of Merrimack Valley (1995-2002)

After my experience at the Fashion Institute, another good friend came to my rescue. He was the chairman of the board of the United Way. He signed me up as a volunteer, primarily to get me out of the house. I was thankful that he did so, as it became a very enriching experience. After some years, I suggested a number of improvements for the operation. The next thing I knew, I had become the president. During my tenure, I visited all fifty-four of the agencies the United Way supported and discovered three basic facts. First, these non-profit social agencies spent most of their money and efforts on service to people. Little effort or money was spent on the business side. The professionals in these agencies see the great demand for their services and, because of this, in comparison, the business side becomes an insignificant part of the operation. For example, the director of a well-respected agency tried to keep the agency going by using her credit card to finance the operation to the tune of $20,000. The United Way helped to keep the agency afloat by facilitating a merger with another agency and, fortunately, this worked out well. Overall, the personnel at non-profits are devoted to their work. They certainly don't do it to make money, but really for the satisfaction of helping others. However, it would certainly help if more people with business experience would get involved. A second major discovery for me was how little I knew about the widespread needs that exist in our own backyard of Merrimack Valley. Our country often looks down on socialism. However, the system that we have in place, largely dependent on the volunteer system to help those who cannot help themselves, is inadequate from what I observed. The third problem that I recognized was that many United Way branches were too small to be able to provide the necessary means to operate effectively. Fortunately, the national offices have initiated some consolidation of small operations and have also concentrated their help on agencies dealing with youth.

The Asian Center of Merrimack Valley (2003-2006)

In 2003, I was contacted by Sister Elana, who was affiliated with the Sisters of Charity. She had retired as a teacher and become the director of the Asian Center. This organization was an outreach of the Archdiocese of Boston. The purpose of the operation was to help Asian immigrants to get a good start in the US. She explained that she didn't have much experience with the business end of the center and was not able to get adequate help from the archdiocese. She wanted to have an independent agency and asked for my help. Sister Elana was a very impressive woman who truly practiced what she believed and had an open mind about religion in general. Since I belonged to a Congregational Church and had never worked with a nun, I carefully assessed whether we could work constructively together. I felt that we could work well together and our collaboration proved to work out far beyond my expectations. She was truly an inspiration for me.

We were able to separate from the archdiocese with their blessing. We became an IRS-approved non-profit organization. Sister Elana had been very frugal and conservative in handling money matters, so the new independent agency was off to a good start. We were able to get people with the needed expertise and maturity to form a productive board. The challenges of helping immigrants to become productive citizens are quite complicated. Many people had endured extreme cruelty and danger. They had come from a totally different culture. One horror story concerned a family that included a sister who had been buried alive by the Khmer Rouge. She was rescued by her brother, who was hiding in a tree while the ordeal took place. After the criminals left, he dug her out. She, however, was injured for life. Some immigrants came together as a family including grandparents, parents and children.

Each generation needed different types of support to assimilate and feel comfortable with our life style. Almost all of them had lost their belongings and were very poor. Sister Elana dealt so effectively with these people with different religions and problems with the English language. We were able to make the agency effective and productive. I was blessed to be a part of it and became a close friend of Sister Elana. After three years, both the Sister Elana and I retired. She wanted to pursue a new career and moved to Nova Scotia. Tragically, in early 2009, while she was driving, a car driving in the opposite direction apparently tried to avoid hitting an animal on the road and crashed head-on into her car and she was killed. It was a great tragedy. It is rare, and I feel blessed to have had a chance to become friends and work with a person who truly lived completely and solely to help others.

Reflections

At age 85, I still host a TV show and invite interesting people for a discussion, give speeches and play the piano in a jazz band. I also sing in a choir, am active in my church and participate in Rotary and on the board of Hillview Montessori School.

I realize that both my early youth and the teenage experiences during the extremes of World War II have made a lasting impact on my life. I became very sensitive to human suffering and have a deep appreciation for the great ideas of our forefathers to build a government with four independent entities checking on each other. Our democracy, built over the years by people from all over the world, from different cultures and persuasions, has grown, despite all the imperfections of mankind, into a country where people can be heard, live and prosper in freedom. Because of that sensitivity, I feel almost a compulsion to sort out the major issues in our society and do the little I can—to discuss and point out where the pitfalls are and what we can do about them. Of course, the major issues are so complex that no human being can even have a fraction of understanding of what it takes to resolve major issues in our present global society.

I have given many speeches, especially to middle school and up to college-level students, but also to adults about what makes a democracy. I was once addressing an audience of World War II veterans. Before my speech, I was seated at a table with a veteran and his wife. She told me that her husband had never shared with her his experiences while fighting in Europe, no matter how much she had encouraged him to do so. I started my speech with an emotional introduction, explaining that I noticed at these meetings that Americans were thanking Americans for fighting Hitler. I told them that I personally wanted to thank them, as a Dutchman, for having saved my life and so many others. When I returned to my table, both the man and his wife were crying. She told me that her husband was so moved that he told her that it was time to tell her about his war experiences.

I realize that it is very difficult, especially for young people, to see how lucky we are to live in a democracy. Unfortunately, from my many talks with young and old, there is not enough attention given to what the obligations are for each individual living in a democracy. Serious conversations about issues are not common. Our educational system concentrates mostly on skills to get a good job. The arts, which really provide true images of life and promote creative thinking, play a secondary role and are often the first educational offerings to be cut. Though we have a multiplicity of religions, all seem to agree on the importance of caring, sharing, and high standards of ethics. They all try to influence our society to aim for these lofty goals, but have not been very effective. Instead, what do we see? "What's in it for me? Materialism creates happiness." As one comedian puts it, "We are in the race to constantly get more stuff". I think that we all need a wakeup call. I sincerely hope that relating some of the horrors of World War II and the advantages I had living in the USA gives all of us food for thought to really do whatever is possible as individuals to preserve our democracy with a better life for all over the world.

ABOUT THE AUTHOR

Jim Vanderpol was born in the Netherlands. A normal childhood turned into one of terror when Nazi Germany occupied his country. He survived the war, and, then with his older brother Maurice (Ries) came to the United States. After graduating from Rider College and earning his CPA, he entered the world of business. Some of the organizations he served were Coopers and Lybrand, public accountants and Becton Dickinson, a large medical instrument company.

He later entered the educational field as V.P. of Finance and Administration at Bennington College in Vermont, Bradford College in Haverhill, Massachusetts and Emerson College in Boston, Massachusetts.

Because retirement was not his cup of tea, he became engaged as a consultant at The Fashion Institute of New York and later on at the United Way of Merrimack Valley where he became the President.

He resides in Plaistow, New Hampshire with his wife Carol, a cat, Oliver, and has seven large koi in a fish pond he built. He also keeps busy as a producer of a local TV show and is the piano "guy" with a jazz band. In addition, he gives speeches about his war experiences, especially to young people.